TEXT TECHNOLOGIES

TEXT
TECHNOLOGIES

A History

Elaine Treharne and Claude Willan

STANFORD UNIVERSITY PRESS
Stanford, California

STANFORD UNIVERSITY PRESS
Stanford, California

LIBRARY OF CONGRESS CATALOGING-IN-PUBLICATION DATA
Names: Treharne, Elaine M., author. | Willan, Claude, author.
Title: Text technologies : a history / Elaine Treharne and Claude Willan.
Description: Stanford, California : Stanford University Press, 2020. |
    Series: Stanford text technologies | Includes bibliographical references and index.
Identifiers: LCCN 2019010215 (print) | LCCN 2019013548 (ebook) |
    ISBN 9781503604513 (electronic) | ISBN 9781503600485 (cloth : alk. paper) |
    ISBN 9781503603844 (pbk. : alk. paper)
Subjects: LCSH: Communication—History. | Communication—Social aspects. |
    Communication—Technological innovations.
Classification: LCC P90 (ebook) | LCC P90 .T69 2019 (print) | DDC 302.209—dc23
LC record available at https://lccn.loc.gov/2019010215

Cover design by Rob Ehle

Text design by Kevin Barrett Kane

Typeset at Stanford University Press in 10/15 Spectral

CONTENTS

ILLUSTRATIONS

PREFACE

This book supports any introductory pedagogic or scholarly activity in areas loosely labeled as Bibliography, the History of the Book, the History of Information or Communication, the History of Science, Manuscript Studies, or the History of Text Technologies, and it can be usefully employed in textually based digital humanities work. By carefully explaining the field, clearly examining terminology and themes, and providing illustrated and pertinent case studies, students and teachers can generate multiple investigations into and debates about how human communication—its production, form and materiality, reception, and cultural value—is crucial to any analysis and interpretation of cultures, history, and societies.

Our categories and definitions are designed to be tested and evaluated. We invite student readers to devise their own categories for the second- and third-level concepts and trends. For those who study the history of text technologies, we suggest that the highest conceptual order is fixed (intentionality, materiality, functionality, and cultural value) and pertains to all text technologies. The second order has some flexibility, but the third order, and others subsumed beneath that, are capacious and can be filled out with themes and approaches specific to the work that each reader and course is doing. As well as providing the basis for the study of the history of text technologies, the concepts and themes identified throughout this book are useful for the new field of predictive text technologies, as the development of forms and methods of human communication seems to be very much a cyclical process. Supplementary materials and suggestions for additional text technologies case studies can be found at https://texttechnologies.stanford.edu/.

ACKNOWLEDGMENTS

The study and teaching of the history of text technologies started with a program at Florida State University (FSU), founded conceptually by Rick Emmerson, Stan Gontarski, Gary Taylor, Lori Walters, and Wayne Wiegand. The first new members of that program included English Department colleagues A. E. B. Coldiron, Paul Fyfe, David Gants, Elizabeth Spiller, and Elaine Treharne. Close working relationships with special collections librarians at FSU proved critical to the successful teaching of courses, and particular gratitude is owed to Sammie Morris (to whom thanks are also due for help in acquiring permissions for images), Bill Modrow, and Ben Yadon.

Subsequently, the two of us have taught Text Technologies at Stanford University, and one of us, Elaine Treharne, is the director of the Stanford Text Technologies enterprise (https://texttechnologies.stanford.edu/), supported by the Roberta Bowman Denning Fund, and CyberText Technologies, supported by the Hewlett Foundation through Stanford's Cyber Initiative. This book is the work of the last seven years of teaching and learning from students in text technologies courses and thinking hard about the issues of the intentionality, materiality, and functionality of all forms of human communication and about their cultural and historical value. This thinking has benefited from the input of many researchers, including Matt Aiello, Celena Allen, Jessica Beckman, Ben Diego, Steele Douris, Dan Kim, H. B. Klein, and Clare Tandy.

Elaine Treharne particularly thanks Benjamin Albritton, John Mustain, Tim Noakes, Roberto Trujillo, and Rebecca Wingfield at Stanford University Libraries; Andrew Prescott at the University of Glasgow; and Greg Walker at the University of Edinburgh. Research in text technologies is facilitated and supported by colleagues at Stanford's Center for Spatial and Textual Analysis, to whom the authors are grateful.

Claude Willan especially thanks Elaine Treharne, who was a model of collegiality throughout this book's gestation. For their support, probing, questioning, and help, he is also particularly grateful to Mark Algee-Hewitt, Jean Bauer, and the staff of the Princeton Center for Digital Humanities; John Bender; Ryan Heuser; Blair Hoxby; Jacob Sider Jost; Lamb; Micha Lazarus; Sophia; Meredith Martin; Gràinne Watson; and his family.

Finally, both authors would like to offer heartfelt thanks to Alan Harvey, Leah Pennywark, Gigi Mark, and all at Stanford University Press for their expert guidance, helpful advice, and admirable patience.

TEXT TECHNOLOGIES

PART I   CONCEPTUAL FRAMEWORK

THE FIELD OF TEXT TECHNOLOGIES is a capacious analytical and interpretive framework that focuses on all textual records from the earliest periods of traceable human communication (perhaps as early as 70,000 BCE) to the present. These records can take the form of images, writing, sound, or action, as long as these are meaningful and produced with intentionality by a human agent. Text technologies seeks to discover why, by whom, when, how, for whom, and in what contexts those textual artifacts were produced and to uncover the long history of instantiations of each technology. An investigation of these core components of a textual artifact (any meaningful form of communication that is recorded) demonstrates underlying systems and a unifying structure. It is possible, then, to determine specific trends and concepts emerging through successive cycles of text technological facture the better to understand how communication has operated historically and might operate in the future.

INTRODUCTION TO TEXT

TEXT comprises signs, symbols, or sounds of any kind that intentionally convey meaning.[1] It is a conceptual category with a vast demesne that encompasses all forms of human communication. The signs or symbols that convey and display meaning are by definition physical, perceptible phenomena ranging from systematic markings on rocks to radar blips. This is the crux and the friction at the heart of this book: the idea of text is abstract, but our means of perceiving it is always physical and concrete—what we call technological, rooted in praxis and technē. The conveyance of meaning happens through a technological, nontextual form and necessitates know-how, tools, and a medium or substrate.

TEXT can take many different forms. It could be a chair or a government building (its design, architecture, decorations, or the sum of the subordinate texts into a whole text), as well as more conventional vectors of meaning like advertisements, cartoons, bitcoin, posters, songs, magazines, newspapers, YouTube videos, and books. The technologies involved in making a chair can include joinery, carving, welding, molding, weaving, or upholstering, but in order to read it as TEXT, it must have been produced with the intention of communicating a meaningful message that an audience could usually interpret. As we will see with different texts throughout this book, the most complex chairs are multitechnological hybrids—component technologies working together to form a powerful and multivalent whole. A good example of a distinctive text in this case is a throne or an Eames lounger.

This section introduces and explains our working definition, and taxonomy, of TEXT as a concept, providing multiple examples so that you can recognize which kinds of objects fit into this overarching field and which do not. We then introduce a way to analyze objects that are texts.

Finding and Defining TEXT

Since the meanings of texts are conveyed perceptibly, through physical means, we can refine the definition of TEXT that we just offered to the following: TEXT (or, indeed, a text) is a voluntarily and intentionally human-created phenomenon that contains and imparts an interpretable and meaningful message, accessible to a community of receivers (even if that community is just one person talking to himself or herself).[2] We will go through this definition term by term to provide a working sense of what TEXT can and cannot be.

Voluntariness is an important component of this definition. Emanations of the involuntary physical consequences of having a body in the world, for example, are not TEXT. A sneeze, a shiver, a bruise: these somatic reactions are perceptible phenomena, but they are not TEXT. By the same token, the unintentional side effects of intentional acts are not ordinarily TEXT: the cloud of dust thrown up by a pneumatic drill, the squeak of a door's hinges, the erosion of a riverbank over time. All of these phenomena, if unintended or if without human agency, cannot be TEXT.

This brings us to the next term in the definition: *intentionality*. Intentionality has the ability to frame, or reframe, phenomena into TEXT. Phenomena produced or interpreted under the circumstances of active and directed intentionality can be argued to be TEXT. Stars simply existing in the sky are natural phenomena, for example. When humans understand stars to represent astrological signs or read a star's positioning to detect direction, those stars become TEXT because the human mediator intentionally seeks and interprets meaning.

The presence of the word *intentionality* in the definition thus reflects our anthropocentric approach to TEXT. We do not consider naturally occurring phenomena, in situ, to be TEXT. Under normal circumstances, phenomena that occur without active or conscious human intervention—the shaping of driftwood, weather events, a rock—are not TEXT. Even if human actions affect our perception of these phenomena (e.g., altered tidal patterns, global warming, mining), they are not TEXT. And even when these phenomena are used as component parts of a text (driftwood as art in a home, depiction of storms or twisters in a news broadcast or a film, use of rocks in garden displays), the underlying natural physical objects are not in themselves TEXT, even though they are component parts of TEXT.

In sum, intentionality is the deliberateness or agency behind a text's creation, inspiring its production. An author's intentionality is her willful bringing into being of meaningful communication. A scribe's intentionality might be his wish to create a regulated, calligraphically expert piece of writing. Bing Crosby's crooning, developed through careful use of sound recording in the 1940s, intentionally attempted to create an intense closeness to a distant, unknown, and unknowable audience.

Interpretable is the corollary term to *created* in this definition: if a human agent must make the text, then that agent must also perceive it. Here we capture the essentially communicative function of TEXT. Even intentionally created phenomena that leave no physical or mental trace for others to discover cannot be, for the purposes of text technologies, TEXT. Thoughts that pass through one's head that are never expressed are, in effect, self-perceptible, but in order to be called TEXT, the phenomena usually need to be perceptible and interpretable to some communicatee. This is a tricky area, though. If I speak to myself and have an entire interior conversation, this is, to all intents and purposes, TEXT. However, if I then leave no record or make no summary of this interior conversation, it is as if it never happened and the functionality or potential interpretability of that silent utterance is voided.

Our use of the word *phenomenon* reflects our belief that texts are first and foremost experiential in their nature. TEXT can generally be studied by others only because in its broadest and most capacious sense, it can be experienced by others; metaphysical, noumenal objects are beyond the scope of this discipline.[3] An abstract concept such as justice, for example, could never, in and of itself, be TEXT, however much other texts might address it.

Describing TEXT
To accurately describe TEXT, we have developed a core triad of concepts that might be thought of as the structure of all text technologies. Any text can be taxonomized using this triad:

Intentionality
Materiality
Functionality

Each of these concepts is addressed in this part. But a shortcut to understand how the triad applies to a text is to ask yourself:

1. What was this text intended to do? [intentionality]
2. What is this text made of? What does it look like? What are its component parts? What is it composed of, and what objects were used to make it? [materiality]
3. What does this text actually do? How does it perform in the real world? What is its biography or long history? [functionality]

With this rubric in hand, describing a text seems simpler than deciding whether something is or is not TEXT in the first place. Like all neat distinctions, however, the truth is more complex. In practice, each of these components will interfere with the pure working of the other two. A text's materiality will inevitably have an impact on how we understand its functionality (and here, we are talking about individual texts, so we move from the semantic, and abstract, field of TEXT). Its intentionality will skew our perception even of its materiality, and while the intentionality behind the creation of a text might remain stable, the materiality of a text can alter dramatically (in the printing of a poem, for example, and its oral delivery to a live audience). To this triad, we have added the concept of cultural value, an inescapable component that evades easy definition but is at work in all cases with varying degrees of predominance: a paper napkin with a child's drawing may have a minuscule degree of cultural value (in this case, sentimental value for the child's parents perhaps), but when John Lennon scribbles lyrics for a new Beatles song on a napkin, that textual object has immense cultural and financial value.

Thus, every individual text and individual text technology in this book can be anatomized with the triad *plus or minus* cultural value to reveal internal tensions and compromises, suggest how each of those factors enhances and undermines the text's effectiveness, and elucidate the significance of one factor over the others.

$$\text{TEXT} = \text{intentionality} + \text{materiality} + \text{functionality} +/- \text{cultural value}$$

One can consider this full interpretation of a text, or text in its widest sense, to be plenitextual.[4]

WHAT IS THE STUDY OF TEXT TECHNOLOGIES?

Students who are new to text technological studies might be wondering at this point how this approach is distinguishable from disciplines that might be more familiar to them, such as literary studies or history. First, we'll offer two rough thumbnail sketches of those disciplines and then show how and where text technologies differs.

History is the search for an ever more inclusive set of reconstructions of past actions, decisions, and motivations. Historians weigh evidence with a view to creating an ideally even-handed, accurate account of precisely what a now-disappeared version of the world looked like and (sometimes) how that particular moment emerged from, or led to, other now-past moments. The focus of traditional history has been on conjecturing the most plausible version of people and events possible given the evidence available from a variety of records and sources.

Within literary studies, the subdiscipline that most resembles text technologies is book history, a critical practice predicated on the insight that the material forms of a text influence how that text was read and how later texts were written. In a sense, text technologies simply extends this insight to its logical conclusion: it is the long history of the use of technē to encode or mediate signs. But our approach to the study of meaning differs substantially from that undertaken in most literary courses. For example, one considerable difference is that the notion of intention, or intentionality, is central to our understanding of text. Since at least the 1960s, literary scholarship (from Barthes, Derrida, I. A. Richards, and many others) has insisted—for its own purposes, quite rightly—that the literary text is discrete and isolated from its creator. This phenomenon is known loosely as "the death of the author." In the history of text technologies, however, the creator of the text as an agent, whether as an author or copyist or film producer, is a central figure, but the materiality and subsequent history and reception of the text are equally important. In this book, we are concerned with the different methods agents have used to communicate meanings over time and the different ways in which those communications have been received, understood, and valued. Any object that intentionally conveys meaningful and potentially interpretable information is a text technology to be studied.

Whereas literary studies concerns itself first and foremost with the structure, meaning, definitions, and use of communicating objects and history with agents, their actions, and their interactions, text technologies treads a thoroughly hybrid middle ground. In short, text technologies addresses the material history of communications among human agents over the *longue durée*.

HOW TO USE THIS BOOK

This book is divided into four parts. Each part takes a different tack in its exploration of the conceptual, historical, and material history of text technologies. This book is not designed to be read straight through, but for you to flip backward and forward from section to section. The argument of the book is revealed throughout the book and builds over the successive parts, during which you will encounter new concepts, new objects, and new terms, such as the "chemise" (from the French for "shirt") that might cover a nineteenth-century book like the cloth version of a modern dust jacket, for example. If there are terms that are unclear to you, look them up in the *Oxford English Dictionary* (our preferred dictionary) or online.

Undergraduate students who were using this book while it was in preparation found it helpful to write in the book itself, responding to the questions that follow many of the sections, particularly in Part 2. These questions, together with the specifically selected Further Reading lists, are designed to help you think about each section in the wider context of text technologies, as well as stimulate ideas for examples of text technologies that you know fit into the various categories we have offered here.

OVERVIEW OF THIS BOOK

All of the four parts of this book are interdependent, and no one part of the book would give a full and fair representation of text technologies without the other three. The part that you are now reading treats the conceptual framework underpinning text technologies. This framework deals both with first-order concepts crucial to understanding the approach, like the core triad, and with second-order concepts that work to give a finer-grained account of the myriad uses and lives of TEXT as a concept.

Part 2 gives an overview of the history of text technologies, running from cave paintings to Snapchat. As we move through that history, we refer to concepts we articulated in Part 1 while also rooting our text technological examples in specific cases.

We offer a range of case studies in Part 3 to move us out of the laboratory and show TEXT in the wild, as it were, in all its variety, hybridity, and heterogeneity. We believe that the case studies are an important corrective to the technological overview of Part 2, which might on its own suggest not only a uniform progression of technologies over time but that texts are simple, monotechnological phenomena.

We close in Part 4 with a few instances of text technological transformation as a way of teasing out the inertia and impetus that hold back and drive innovation and change: What social forces, in particular, stimulate text technological innovation, and what social transformations are affected by technological innovation? By looking at significant transformations from history, we outline the two mutually exclusive explanations for those transformations: social constructivism and technological determinism.

We hope that this book offers departure points for many different discussions on text technologies and related approaches to the history of the cultural record. We have provided too much material here for any one class to cover, but by breaking the book up into parts covering the conceptual, historical, practical, and transformational facets of text technologies, we offer a fertile and varied source for many different approaches to TEXT.

PRINCIPAL CONCEPTS

Intentionality

The first term in the structure of intentionality, materiality, functionality, and (plus or minus) cultural value relates to two qualities of TEXT. The first is a yes/no question that is, as we have seen, crucial to determining whether an object is a text. Does it have textual intentionality? Was the object created with the intention of communicating something to someone? The very baseline for determining intentionality is assuring the intervention of a human agent in constructing or mediating a phenomenon.

Once this condition has been satisfied, intentionality can have a more nuanced application. Somewhat akin to a historically bound determination of functionality, it consists in posing the question: What was the specific intention of the creator(s) of this text when it was made? What state of affairs in the world did the creator of this text hope to rectify or preserve, celebrate, or mourn? In other words, why did the person create it?

Although intentions are historically determined, they are not historically fluid. The intention of Darius I's self-glorifying inscription at Behistun, for example, is quite unchanged by the subsequent use of the inscription, carved into the side of a mountain, as a site for artillery target practice in World War II. That intentionality will always have been determined by Darius, his architects, and his masons. Similarly, while texts frequently undergo adaptive reuse, there is only one intentional mode in play at any given time: an author will write a literary manuscript in order to state a message or make a contribution to contemporary culture; the publisher will produce a printed version with the intention of transmitting the text to a larger audience. The literary work will be similar in both manifestations, but the producers are different and their intentions, while related, refer specifically to their material productions.

To say that intentionality is a more straightforward component of the triad than functionality is not to say, however, that motivations are ever simple or single. This complexity is often ramified by the collaborative nature of much text. Consider the intentions of only two people involved

FURTHER READING

Barthes, Roland. "The Death of the Author." In *Image, Music, Text*, translated by S. Heath, 142–48. London: Fontana, 1977.

Culler, Jonathan. *The Pursuit of Signs: Semiotics, Literature, Deconstruction*. Ithaca, NY: Cornell University Press, 1981.

Hayles, Katherine N. *Writing Machines*. Cambridge, MA: MIT Press, 2002.

Kant, Immanuel. *The Critique of Judgment*, translated by Werner S. Pluhar. Indianapolis: Hackett, 1987.

———. *Critique of Pure Reason*, edited by Paul Guyer and Allen W. Wood. Cambridge: Cambridge University Press, 1999.

Olson, David. *The World on Paper*. Cambridge: Cambridge University Press, 1996.

Tettegah, Sharon Y., and Safiya Umoja Noble, eds. *Emotions, Technology, and Design*. Amsterdam: Elsevier Academic Press, 2016.

in the painting of the ceiling of the Sistine Chapel. Pope Julius II wanted to glorify God and signify the sheer scale of papal power in renovating the Vatican to compensate for his reputation as a warrior pope and to have a comparable reputation to his predecessors as a patron of the visual arts. Michelangelo Buonarroti, for his part, wanted to glorify God, make enough money to survive, create a comprehensive and cohesive visual sourcebook for Old Testament figures and allegories, and testify to his own extraordinary powers as a painter even while he considered sculpture his true calling. The ceiling of the Sistine Chapel is the product of all of these vectors of intention, and many more.

As an analyst of any text, you will often find it helpful to decide in advance precisely whose intentionality you want to determine.

Materiality

Materiality is the part of the triad that corresponds most closely to the "technology" component of text technology. It is the part that concerns itself with transmission of the text: how it is made in terms of the physical components of the textual object, the tools employed for production, and the know-how involved in using the tools in relation to the materials.

One of the things that we always notice about a text, even if we don't know that we notice it, is what it is, what it is made of. A text's materiality is often almost invisible to us precisely because it seems so obvious to us. To say that a book is made of paper is, to us, unnecessary. This book is made of paper. But what of the material and technological differences between hard- and softcover books? What about books with a higher paper weight (for more heft to the page), rough-cut edges on literary fiction, or large- versus small-format printings? What about books that come with dust jackets, or slipcovers? What about differences in the finish given to paper: photography books have a high-gloss finish on their pages, and literary fiction softcovers often have a matte finish. What about color printing or black and white?

Behind each one of these different options is a long history of technological innovation, all the way from the invention of paper itself, to the development of movable type, the bound codex, durable glue, detailed and high-quality image reproduction, and the methods of mass-producing high-quality glossy color images.

To bring order to the great array of material conditions that a text can have, we employ a distinction between substrate and tool. Both offer fertile grounds for innovation, and each comes with particular mediating qualities. The substrate is the matter or surface or support on which the text is created. In a modern codex, the principal substrate (by mass) is paper. Other materials in the production of a codex include (as above) thread and glue, uniting the gatherings and fixing them to the spine. On a jumbotron, by contrast, the substrate is the complex mesh of electricity, wiring, plastic, metal, and LED lights that display words and numbers.

The tool describes whatever is used to inscribe, stamp, manipulate, stimulate, modify, or otherwise interact with the substrate in order to create a text. Without a tool, the substrate is inert; without a substrate, the tool is inarticulate. On the scoreboard, the tool is the program that sequences the illumination of the lights; on paper, it could be a pen and ink, a pencil, a brush and paint; against stone, it is a mallet and chisel.

Tools and substrates can come in pairs since often they are tailored to one another's distinct properties. For example, a fountain pen has been designed to release predictable and even quantities of ink within a certain bandwidth of speeds of writing on a flexible, somewhat absorbent substrate. So too has pure high-grade cotton writing paper been designed to hold certain amounts of ink in a way that precisely reflects where the metal of the fountain pen touched it, and no further. Try using a fountain pen on greaseproof paper, and the substrate will not hold the ink deposited by the tool. If you used a fountain pen on a tissue, the substrate would be maladapted to the tool in the opposite way: it would hold too much ink. In both cases, the tracks of the fountain pen would be illegible. This goes some way toward explaining the great popularity and longevity of certain ideally matched tools and substrates: the ballpoint pen is a technological innovation that performs acceptably on a great range of substrates. Common printer paper (24 pound bond, 92 brightness, 8.5 by 11 inches) is a substrate that has been scrupulously adapted to be suitable for multiple ink-jet or laser tools.

As a general principle, the more successful a text technology is, the more perfectly adapted tool and substrate are to one another. A successful technology can be fitting for either a great variety of messages or only a few. The codex has enjoyed such tremendous popularity over the past two thousand years because of its flexibility and adaptability; in fact, the term *book* is so capacious that its very polyvalence creates longevity for all text technologies that fall under its name (an e-book, for instance, is highly variable in form; a checkbook is specific, involving key elements designed to reinforce authenticity and collective trust in the efficacy of the textual object). The generic form of the jumbotron is nearly ubiquitous in sports arenas and public spaces because it too is a carefully tailored technology capable of conveying many different messages very effectively.

Successive generations of textual production often happen by substrate and tool leapfrogging each other and driving one another forward. Think about just one focused arc of development of textual production: stone, clay, papyrus, parchment or vellum, paper, xylography, printing, typing, xerography, and digital reproduction. Consider the following questions.

1. What links of tool and substrate do you see between these stages?
2. Look at the time line at the beginning of Part 2. What social structures are implied by each stage of production?
3. Do any of the means of production imply the same social structures?
4. What is the overall trend of these changes?

Functionality

On its face, the question of functionality is a simple one: What does a text do? How does it function in the world? These are in some respects questions that bear on what we might call the content of a text. Questions about content boil down to asking, "What does it say?" or "What does it mean?" This is the place, in other words, to include in your evaluation of a text the words, sentences, and paragraphs on the page; the actions and the figures in the painting; and so on. But the problem with this question is that there are almost as many answers as there are answerers, because the evaluation is subjective. Determining what a text says, means, or does has been the goal of much of the entire history of literary criticism, for example.

In fact, functionality is the most complex and shifting of the components of the triad. It depends in part on intention and materials, but it is also contingent on a myriad of other factors: For what context is the text made? For what constructed audience is the text intended? Is it being consumed in the context for which it was made? Reconstructing the historical context of a text can be crucial to understanding part of its functionality, even when that context is now irrecoverably lost. We can make conjectures about the context surrounding the inscriptions at Behistun, for example, but we cannot enter into, or ever fully conceive of, the world of Persia in 522 BCE.

A text's function is not, however, entirely bound by the historical moment of its creation. One can ask how the form of the text affects its reception. Shakespeare's *Hamlet* is a multitude of different textual experiences, depending, for example, on its reception as live performance in a theater, in a movie theater, or by a reader of an edition (or a digital reproduction of the First Folio). Since these historical moments are so often beyond full reconstruction, it can be just as pertinent to evaluate the current functions—new functions—to which historical texts can be put. For example, the Behistun inscription's original function was to establish and reinforce, in various ways, the authority of Darius I. But as the importance of emphasizing Darius's lineage and martial prowess waned, other factors emerged as significant. Now the inscription has been largely repurposed to support the tourist trade of the city of Kermanshah in western Iran.

Functionality is a concept with considerable fluidity; determinations of materiality can be made with relative certainty, those of intentionality can occasionally be made with some certainty, and functionality is in some ways an emergent property of the combination of the first two components in the structure of text technologies. We say "in some ways" because the way that we understand an object is shaped by a constant tension between what it says and the way it is said. The total effect, "what the text does," is the result of an ever-shifting negotiation between the former, the apparent content of the text, and the latter, which is the result of materials and intention.

The fact that functionality is the always-esoteric product of a variable matrix of factors means that it is often the last item that you can determine when analyzing text.

Cultural Value / Aura

In every taxonomy, there are outlying cases—the miscellaneous section of a filing system, the box marked "other" on a survey. The success of a taxonomy is in making those exceptions cohere as a category with a strong internal logic. In our case, the core equation, the structure, of text technological investigation is enhanced by what we, borrowing a term from Walter Benjamin, call "aura" or, more broadly perhaps, cultural value. In his essay "The Work of Art in the Age of Mechanical Reproduction," Benjamin writes,

> One might subsume the eliminated element in the term *aura* and go on to say: that which withers in the age of mechanical reproduction is the aura of the work of art. This is a symptomatic process whose significance points beyond the realm of art. One might generalize by saying that the technique of reproduction detaches the reproduced object from the domain of tradition.[5]

The aura, then, is something that, according to Benjamin, exists "beyond the realm of art." Aura is not necessarily a predominant part of a text, but it is inextricable from it. Benjamin's essay argues in part that our society is so defined by the mass production of objects and the mass reproduction of images and messages that we have come to fetishize something that we call authenticity. When you go to the National Portrait Gallery in London and look at the famous *Chandos* painting of William Shakespeare, your experience of that text is overwhelmed by your awareness that you are in the physical presence of that endlessly reproduced original. The object that all those reproductions referred back to is now here, in the room, with you. This frisson of having contact with "the real thing" overrides our ability to look at or enjoy the painting on its own terms and entraps us instead in an exciting feeling of having in some way transcended our ordinary lives. When you go to see the *Chandos* Shakespeare, all you will usually see is its aura—its value to our culture as one of a long line of cultures that have appreciated the painting.

The ironies of this are many; most prominent, by experiencing aura or cultural value above the other three components of a text, you are contained once again within the ordinary life that you feel you have transcended. After all, the sensation of aura is about you and your bodily presence, not about an act of textual communication. Second, using many online art repositories, you can now examine a text like the Shakespeare portrait with far more attention to its functionality, intentionality, and materiality than you ever could in person; it can be seen in much greater detail than would be possible within its actual physical setting

Aura or cultural value is an inescapable fact of our encounters with TEXT. And Benjamin's definition of aura as a predicament that we were saddled with by the culture industry is not the only definition. Some technologies were developed entirely to cater to the projection of aura—saints' reliquaries, for example, which hold fragmented or whole physical remnants of those deemed to be holy by the Catholic Church. Other kinds of aura and cultural prioritization are possible wherever the perceiving agent finds or ascribes a noumenal quality such as value, beauty, the aesthetic, authenticity, and so on in a text that they consider key to its operation but cannot account for without recourse to something beyond the triad of function, intention, and materiality. Indeed, you could argue that the presence of aura/cultural value of some kind is what makes a text worth analyzing in the first place. The question that aura prompts us to ask ourselves is this: How much of a text can we attribute to the intentionality, materiality, and functionality, and how much must we consent simply never to understand?

SECONDARY CONCEPTS

We offer here a set of secondary functions that can be found in TEXT. These concepts or functions are neither necessary nor sufficient for determining whether something is a text. This set is not exhaustive, and the concepts here are not exclusive; they can be combined with one another endlessly. Rather, we imagine the following concepts to be a sampling of conceptual operations that a text might perform or depend on. Readers should add new concepts or functions that they discern in texts they study to this list as they see fit and combine and recombine different operations in as many different ways as they please. These second-order concepts are presented as an expansive matrix through which TEXT might move, and with which an individual text might be analyzed.

Sedimentation

Sedimentation is a term to describe the way that users respond to a new text technology. Sometimes we use the new tool and substrate to make and consume a text in familiar ways. When text technological innovation comes in advance of social demand for that innovation, only slowly do we explore the possibilities for making and consuming any text that the new technology offers us.

For example, when movable type was first used in western Europe in the middle of the fifteenth century, books that were produced were finished by hand and made to look like the manuscripts that had been created for many centuries before. Working within the idea of what is familiar and in order to maintain audiences' desire for the book-object they knew and trusted, printers like Johannes Gutenberg and William Caxton also drew on the design of manuscripts in their typefaces and page layout. Indeed, Timothy Barrett at the University of Iowa Center for the Book notes that early papermakers in Europe sometimes finished the making of their product by sizing the paper with melted gelatin to create a substrate that essentially felt and smelled like parchment or vellum. The type, the layout, the hand-finished initials, and the sizing in these early years of Western printing created books that are perfect examples of a hybrid text technology—the sedimentation of successive technologies that demonstrate the gradual evolution of one technology into another. In contemporary electronic text technologies, this incremental process of design and transformation is akin to skeumorphism (a design feature where components of a technology are made to look like the things they represent in real life—for example, the "notes" icon on an iPhone, which looks like a yellow notepad).

Sedimentation and skeumorphism deliberately perform a kind of nostalgic work. There are apps for the iPad that replace its interface with a representation of a typewriter. This allows you to use the iPad in a distinctly sedimented way, even though it has been painstakingly engineered to be very far indeed from that nonelectrical mechanical object with a ribbon, ink, and a bell. The fact that our phones and tablets still rely on representations of keyboards as their principal mode of input is only in part because of the shortcomings of voice-recognition software; it is also because it makes users feel more comfortable with a new substrate to be able to use a familiar, sedimented tool on it.

A more text-based example of sedimentation can be seen in email: sedimented users of email still often write emails as though they were letters. Writing "Dear Emily" at the start of an email is necessary only if someone else in Emily's household might see the letter, to indicate that the letter is only for Emily. In the same way, signing off "Yours sincerely, James" is necessary only if the recipient has no other way of recognizing James's identity. In email, the To: and From: fields obviate the need for these conventions, but users may stick to them out of an unconscious habit or a determination that they believe an email to be like a letter, thus priding themselves on their deliberate sedimentation.

Whether voluntary or involuntary, sedimentation is an index of anxiety. The greater our anxiety about a text technology and the greater the perceived potential for the technology to undermine us by speaking in a way that we cannot control or understand or even perceive, the more heavily sedimented our use of it will be.

Conversely, the technologies that are perceived to be the most socially accepted among particular groups will have the least sedimentation and will also see the greatest testing of technological boundaries. Which

FURTHER READINGS

Crick, Julia, and Alexandra Walsham, eds. *The Uses of Script and Print, 1300–1700*. Cambridge: Cambridge University Press, 2004.

Smith, Margaret M. "Red as a Textual Element during the Transition from Manuscript to Print." In *Textual Cultures: Cultural Texts, Essays and Studies*, edited by Orietta Da Rold and Elaine Treharne, 187–200. Woodbridge, UK: D. S. Brewer, 2010.

technologies these are change with time and innovation. For hundreds of years, the letter was used in a markedly nonsedimented way. For example, in the nineteenth century, the cross-hatched, or simply "crossed," letter, which overlaid multiple layers of handwritten text at different angles on a single sheet of paper to maximize the content the substrate could carry, was a sign that the letter was, for those users, a completely naturalized technology with no potential costs attached for fluent or innovative use. Similarly, users who Tweet or text with abbreviations, emojis, or acronyms or who substitute numbers for letters are signaling that they fear no social cost to exploiting the confines of the technology. Users who refuse to bend their text to the text technology signal a belief that the higher potential cost of communicating their familiarity with that technology outweighs any potential benefits of that act of textual and technological innovation.

With these examples we can see that sedimentation reveals a profound truth about a text and text technologies, more broadly: not only are they essentially social because they allow us to communicate with one another, but any use of a text technology is a socially fraught and freighted act.

Spend some time with these questions:

1. How can you predict sedimentation?
2. Can you give a few examples in your everyday life of sedimentation in action?
3. Why might you want to use a sedimented text technology in certain cases?
4. What nonutilitarian effects might that use have?

Authority

We have mentioned the signature. Whether in relation to email, a check, a license, a contract or passport, a letter, or an artwork, the signature is still one of our strongest signifiers of authority. Authority has many meanings for text technological studies. How might a text claim to be authoritative, and how might it resist such a claim? There are two kinds of authority particularly tightly interwoven in a text: the sense of authority as truthfulness, accuracy, or verisimilitude (epistemological authority) and the sense of authority as power (temporal authority).

If a text makes the claim of authenticity, what can we infer about the purpose of the text? How does a text authorize, or authenticate, itself? Is there something in the substrate itself that demonstrates authority—a fingerprint, watermark, or digital watermark, for example? Is there something real about the materiality of the text in relation to its physical context (the strokes of a paintbrush, correct inks for the period, an untampered binding)? Is something added to the textual object (a seal, a stamp, a certificate)? Or is there something in how it is disseminated (a public address system, a broadcast from the White House, a specialist auction)?

Our introduction of authority at this point builds on the key insight gained while thinking through sedimentation: a text is social. A text is social, and social bodies (in order to be perceived as such) require organization; organization requires authority, whether epistemological or temporal. It is therefore impossible to divorce TEXT and text technological innovation from tension or anxiety around the concept of authority, whichever way that authority is understood.

In our remarks on sedimentation, we hinted at the anxiety that older generations may typically feel about the text technological innovations of younger generations. Newspapers and magazines regularly wax millenarian about how new forms of TEXT are undermining life as we know it and changing it irrevocably for the worse. It's instructive when confronted with these dire predictions to consult no less authoritative and ancient a source than Plato. In this extract from Plato's *Phaedrus*, Socrates is telling a story. In this story, the god Thamus is remonstrating with the god Theuth (or Thoth), who had invented writing:

Now in those days the god Thamus was the king of the whole country of Egypt. . . . To him came Theuth and showed his inventions, desiring that the other Egyptians might be allowed to have the benefit of them; he enumerated them, and Thamus enquired about their several uses, and praised some of them and censured others, as he approved or disapproved of them. . . . This, said Theuth, will make the Egyptians wiser and give them better memories; it is a specific both for the memory and for the wit. Thamus replied: O most ingenious Theuth, the parent or inventor of an art is not always the best judge of the utility or inutility of his own inventions to the users of them. And in this instance, you who are the father of letters, from a paternal love of your own children have been led to attribute to them a quality which they cannot have; for this discovery of yours will create forgetfulness in the learners' souls, because they will not use their memories; they will trust to the external written characters and not remember of themselves. The specific which you have discovered is an aid not to memory, but to reminiscence, and you give your disciples not truth, but only the semblance of truth; they will be hearers of many things and will have learned nothing; they will appear to be omniscient and will generally know nothing; they will be tiresome company, having the show of wisdom without the reality.[6]

As this famous passage shows, apocalyptic concerns about intellectual decay are, ironically, evergreen. Thamus's remarks about the effect of writing on future learners are remarkably close to any number of hand-wringing op-eds about the deleterious effects of digital text technologies on classroom learning or on the way a child's brain functions. It is perhaps not a coincidence that Thamus uses the analogy of parents and children, since text technological shifts engender such specifically intergenerational anxieties. Whether or not they have a corollary in empirical evidence, these worries spring from social causes. When print emerged in Western culture, similar concerns about its ability to proliferate (without any obvious control) were articulated, and it's interesting to consider how much social anxiety that is focused on new text technologies is really about the ability of the "masses" to access information without the mediation of some kind of authority or intervening expertise.

The example from Plato crystallizes an important point, then: text technologies and innovations in those technologies are themselves a vector for social control and dissent. To put it more concretely, changes to the materiality of a text, through innovations in substrate or tool, have ramifications for intentionality and functionality that can transform a text and its social operations entirely.

To help think through the complex knot of issues surrounding the many different kinds of authority in texts, here are two contrasting examples with questions to consider:

FURTHER READING
Minnis, A. J. *Medieval Theory of Authorship: Scholastic Literary Attitudes in the Later Middle Ages.* Philadelphia: University of Pennsylvania Press, 1988.

1. The triumphal arch has a very long history as a tradition of architecture that makes certain claims about its builders. It is possible to pick a triumphal, or victory, arch (anywhere from Baghdad to Paris to London) and think about what sort of authority it claims. For example, the Arch of Constantine in Rome was dedicated in 315 to celebrate the victory of the Emperor Constantine at Milvian Bridge. How does it claim authority, and what kind of authority does it represent? To whom is this text designed to communicate, and what function does it serve?

2. Now think about a shopping list. Does a shopping list make any claims to authority? How do you know? Is a shopping list even a text? If so, what kind of text is it? What do your findings imply about the nature of TEXT?

3. From the two examples in questions 1 and 2, what can be deduced about the relationship between private/public and authority?

4. What happens when a text questions the relationship between the two kinds of power?

5. Is material innovation always subversive?

Production, Transmission, Consumption

We've seen how all texts are communicative. The first-order concepts laid out above govern the workings of texts at the highest possible conceptual levels, and these second-order concepts relate to their more prosaic, concrete operations. A secondary triad that describes the life cycle of a text can be proposed and is most commonly deployed in traditional book historical approaches. Using this secondary triad should be helpful in teasing apart the different stages through which a text moves. This triad is as follows:

Production
Transmission
Consumption

These three terms could be reframed as three questions to ask of a text in its lifestyle. How is it made? How does it get from maker to user? And how is it used or consumed? By conceptualizing the movement of a text through these three phases, we can see a narrower version of our core triad of functionality, intentionality, and materiality at work.

Production

By *production* we mean the physical manufacture of a text.[7] To describe the production of a text, then, is to describe in detail the way that the communicating agent manipulates the tool and the substrate. Here is a very simple instance of describing the production phase of a text technology. Pressure and motion are applied by the user's hand to a small cylindrical fragment of calcium sulphate or carbonate on a dark, hard, flat, matte, or nonreflective surface (in its earliest forms, this substrate was a sheet of slate). That pressure and manipulation can leave a series of highly legible marks, from which a producer can make a text.

This is how chalk gets onto a blackboard. This example shows how much we take for granted in text technologies that with which we are familiar: we might know what a piece of chalk looks like and feels like and how to use it. We might also know other nontextual side effects of that tool, like the dust it leaves on the hands and clothes of the user. But to describe the production side of the text technology fully requires great attention to detail and a degree of defamiliarization from a technology that we have more or less naturalized.

Transmission

Texts are usually intended to be consumed by at least one agent more than the number of agents who produced it. Transmission is how an agent disseminates a text: How does it get from the maker to the user? Modes of transmission depend heavily on the form and the substrate used for the text. Some forms and substrates are portable; some are not. Many forms (e.g., monuments, warning signs, projector screens on walls) are static and meant to exist permanently in public places. Some forms and substrates move themselves, some need to be moved, and some need to stay put. All three models apply to different sorts of texts.

Here is how we could describe the transmission phase of the text technology we just described in production: the chalk and blackboard. In the majority of instances, this substrate is static and fixed to (or in some cases is even a part of) one or more walls of a room that has been designed to optimize the display of the text. In some cases, the board can be moved on a track or a rail to display multiple boards adjacent to one another. Sometimes wheels are affixed to the base of the board so as to transport it to other rooms. These modes of movement, however, do not under any circumstances describe the transmission phase of this technology: transmission always occurs through the prominent visual display of the text technology to a room from one of that room's walls.

When we describe the transmission phase of this technology, we can see what this substrate has in common with other text technologies, like projectors and screens, posters, whiteboards, and some visual and plastic arts. Most notably, in the case of this substrate, the movement necessary to disseminate the text is made by the users rather than the makers, whose blank substrate awaits the potential of texts that are arguably ephemeral and time-bound in their display.

A useful question to consider now arises from the time lines in Part 2. From these, we can think about how texts have been disseminated from cave paintings to the present day. How have the processes of disseminating a text changed over time? Reflect on the following questions:

FURTHER READING

Darnton, Robert. "What Is the History of Books?" *Daedalus* 111, no. 3 (1982): 65–83.

Derrida, Jacques. *Dissemination,* translated by Barbara Johnson. Chicago: University of Chicago Press, 1983.

Lotte Hellinga, *Texts in Transit: From Manuscript to Proof and Print in the Fifteenth Century.* Brill, Leiden, 2014.

1. What is the connection between modes of, and extents of, transmission and authority?
2. What assumptions can you make, across different technologies, about the intentionality of a text and its claims to authority based on its mode of transmission?
3. What social structures are inherent in different forms of transmission?
4. What does "transmission" mean to different agents?
5. How is the transmission of a text controlled, and what does that control reveal about the social function of that text?

Consumption

The final term in this trio of production, transmission, and consumption concerns what happens to a text after it reaches its audience. Once a text has been produced and transmitted, it comes to a user or consumer. While transmission has its closest technological links to materiality in the core model, consumption is also connected to the other two terms, particularly functionality.

Here is how we might describe the consumption phase of a text on a blackboard. Users congregate in line of sight of the substrate and its text. Many users can consume this text at the same time. Typically users sit and try to learn the text on the text technology that they can see. To help them do this, they often require access to auxiliary text technologies of their own, such as laptops or a pen and paper. While this act of consumption may be pleasurable, it is not designed to be. The design of this often involuntary form of consumption is to maximize the visibility of the same text to the maximum number of consumers possible at one time.

In this way, analyzing the consumption phase of a text technology often reveals the social forms in which that technology is embedded. For example, the consumption phase of the blackboard reveals it to be a substrate well adapted to didactic ends and to be deeply embedded in the social forms that are commensurate with didacticism—forms like schools and the educational establishment (and the corollary notions like that of an organized community reproducing itself with a degree of uniformity enforced through authority) or the idea of a syllabus. The model of consumption required by the blackboard (or to which the blackboard has adapted) is compatible only with settled, literate, relatively peaceful, and stable social forms that are themselves founded on the reliable and regulated consumption of TEXT.

As we can see, analyzing the last phase of the life cycle of a text technology leads us to evaluate the myriad social contexts surrounding that technology. And so using this secondary triad of production, transmission, and consumption, we can build on our earlier insight that a text is always social to suggest this: the forms of production, transmission, and consumption of a text mirror, or create, corresponding social forms.

Censorship

Censorship is part of the family of secondary embedded characteristics of technologies, along with copyright, consortia, and cryptography; these are all social conditions that commonly arise surrounding the production, transmission, and consumption of a text. (Other characteristics could be added here, such as the inherent features of portability or capacity. These are based principally on materiality. Yet other characteristics, such as accessibility or scalability, are also deeply interesting and worth reflecting on.)

Censorship is a name for the interference in a text of a nonproducing agent anywhere in its life cycle. This interference is usually designed to control the text in some way that makes it less subversive to an authority that the interfering agent belongs to or protects. A censor can interfere with the production, transmission, or consumption of a text.

Censorship necessitates at least three distinct agents: one producing the text, one censoring it, and one whose consumption the censor anticipates and regulates. Only fairly sophisticated, centralized, and bureaucratized social forms permit (or indeed necessitate) censorship, since an insight necessary for the development of censorship is one we have already developed: that the forms of text technologies mirror and anticipate social forms and even create new social forms. Since authority regulates social forms, censorship protects the interests of an authority by preventing any text

FURTHER READING

McElligot, Jason. *Royalism, Print and Censorship in Revolutionary England*. Woodbridge, UK: Boydell and Brewer, 2007.

Taranto, James. "Censorship, Inc." *Wall Street Journal*, January 22, 2010. https://www.wsj.com/articles/SB10001424052748704509704575019260028244470.

Banned Books Week: http://www.bannedbooksweek.org/.

Index on Censorship, a journal devoted to tracking all censorship, worldwide: http://bit.ly/19gW0T9.

from performing anything with the potential to be socially innovative.

Some kinds of text technologies are more susceptible to censorship than others, and it is worthwhile considering the kinds of texts that are particularly resistant to censorship. Similarly, some of the three stages of a text technology's life cycle are easier to control than others. Can you think of technologies that evolved specifically to counter censorship? By looking through the examples in this book, what is the earliest text that one can argue might have been subject to censorship, and why? (See the "How to Use This Book" section previously in this chapter. This is an invitation to do as we suggest there and go looking.)

It's also worth considering the different technological forms that censorship itself has taken, from the Vatican's *Index Librorum Prohibitorum*, the UK government's move to censor online pornography, the Christian Family League's list of banned books, books banned from American libraries in different states, age limits on films and computer games, the laws prohibiting graffiti, and censored words in recordings.

Consider these questions:

1. How does censorship drive innovation in text technologies?
2. What text technologies mentioned throughout this book might have developed in response to the pressure exerted by censorship?
3. Which technologies are the easiest, or the hardest, to censor, and why might this be the case?

Copyright

Copyright is another way of regulating text. Like censorship, it can be used to control any of the three stages of a text's life cycle. It is also a mechanism designed to control the passage of a text on behalf of an absent authority—in this case, the copyright holder for a text.

One of the earliest forms of copyright in Great Britain was the Stationer's Register (1557–1710). This was a series of huge volumes in which clerks at the Stationer's Office in London recorded the names of those who had the right to print or perform a text. These records had the force of law in regulating who had the right to print a text. Copyright could be bought from the owners listed in the volume, and the volume was a legally admissible document to prove breach of copyright in court.

Copyright has changed substantially since its embryonic form in the Stationer's Register. Texts once considered common property, like folk tunes, have now become private property in the same way that land that was one held in common is now privately held. For example, one of the most universally known songs, "Happy Birthday to You," was copyrighted and owned by the Warner Music Group until a land-mark ruling in early 2016 that deemed the copyright not to extend to all versions and uses of the song. Until this ruling, in order to embed this song in any commercially distributed text, a producer had to pay a license fee to the Warner Music Group. Until the 2016 ruling, Warner owned the copyright to, and collected $2 million in annual fees from, the use of "Happy Birthday to You." Warner expected to own the song until 2030 and most likely expected to own the copyright to the song until arguments for the next extension on the term of copyright in a court of law.

It is a particular quirk of the professions that oversee the practice of law and those that produce, own, and transmit content that copyright in the United States is continually being extended. A graphic by Tom Bell*, gives a sense of the steadily increasing terms of copyright. Under the 1998 Sonny Bono Copyright Term Extension Act, copyright terms now typically last more than 100 years.

The two shadow forms that copyright gives rise to are piracy and pla-giarism, and these two converses reveal the twin interests that copyright supposedly protects. Piracy denotes illegitimate transmission and con-sumption that harms professional transmitters and creators; publishers, distributors, or creators lose out on potential sales. Plagiarism denotes illegitimate production that harms professional creators—producers of text like writers or musicians, whose productions are used without their permission and who lose out on both financial and creative credit accru-ing from the transmission and consumption of their work.

FURTHER READING

Johns, Adrian. *Piracy: The Intellectual Property Wars from Gutenberg to Gates.* Chicago: University of Chicago Press, 2009.

Rose, Mark. *Authors and Owners: The Invention of Copyright.* Cambridge, MA: Harvard University Press, 1995.

Yglesias, Matt. "Was *Paul's Boutique* Illegal?" *Slate*, May 7, 2012. http://slate.me/16uiln2.

Creative Commons: http://bit.ly/19gVW5L.

Key to copyright terms in the United States: http://bit.ly/15UEork.

* https://commons.wikimedia.org/wiki/File:Tom_Bell%27s_graph_showing_extension_of_U.S._copyright_term_over_time.svg

Consider the following questions:

1. Read the previous paragraph carefully. What social and economic conditions does copyright presume?
2. Would either producers or disseminators ever choose not to enforce their copyrights? Under what circumstances, and why?
3. What challenges does the new ease of dissemination through the internet pose to copyright?
4. Which is the more endangered: intellectual property or copyright? What social and economic forms does each favor? Which do you think is more important?
5. What does the profound division between the two categories say about the influence of text technologies on contemporary civilization?
6. Warner / Chappel Music settled the suit brought against it on the "Happy Birthday to You" copyright for $14 million. Plaintiffs argued successfully that Warner's claim was invalid on several grounds and Warner should return licensing fees "pursuant to their wrongful assertions of copyright." Details of the settlement can be found at https://happybirthdaylawsuit.com/. How does this settlement reflect on the conflicting claims of authority that copyright can bring into play? Which kind of authority won out in this case?

Consortia

Consortia have been a key social formation around text technologies probably from the earliest recorded times. Around the sixth century, monasteries developed writing offices to produce copies of texts, and by the end of the twelfth century, writing shops emerged to produce texts for university students and other consumers, often controlling and commodifying the supply of textual materials. Consortia exist to aid in each stage of the life cycle of a text technology. Writing offices persisted until at least the nineteenth century. The twentieth-century typing pool was a kind of in-house consortium that companies used to generate texts. A print version of the monastic scriptorium was the conger: a loose affiliation of printers who joined together to share the cost of printing and publishing a text. News agencies often work together to produce stories for television and newspapers, but since the emergence of social media like Twitter and Facebook, "news" appears to be a much broader and less controlled category than in previous textual cultures.

Other consortia developed specifically to consume texts. The cultures of discussion in coffeehouses and literary salons were less formalized instances of today's book clubs. Madame de Staël's highly fashionable salon in late eighteenth-century France in some ways performed a function similar to Oprah Winfrey's book club: a congregation of consumers who gather to discuss a text they have all consumed. Because these consuming consortia are convened by a single authority, they are often denigrated by consumers who do not perceive themselves as belonging to a consortium. These consumers, who consider themselves independent, see the convening authorities as having an undue influence on the selection, transmission, and consumption of the text they choose. Still other kinds of consortia exist to collaboratively transmit texts. Contemporary cable companies offer bundles of texts of different kinds; these bundles represent groups of content owners whose commercial interests in the transmission of their texts are aligned.

The internet has seen an enormous burgeoning of consortia. It has produced hybrid consortia that are designed to facilitate both consumption and dissemination. Different online technologies have accentuated different components. MySpace's primary construction as a social network emphasizes the authority of a text's producer, now usually a musician. Flickr is a more pure production/dissemination engine, with less space for the intercession of any authority. Accordingly, sites like Sound-Cloud, Flickr, and Picasa serve more as repositories and archives for texts syndicated from other sources.

While Tumblr has the capacity to showcase producers of texts, it is predominantly designed to facilitate transmission and consumption.

Authority is a secondary consideration on Tumblr; the authority of the Tumblr owner is built up slowly as an aggregate of his or her posts, and the work of transmitters of text is accordingly almost as respected. Pinterest takes authority from aggregate texts to its logical conclusion, and users curate their authority by advertising the text they consume. In this way, Pinterest is the opposite of MySpace.

Consider these questions:

1. What are class associations of different consortia, particularly consumption-based consortia?
2. What social forms persist from scriptoria to Pinterest?
3. What pressures do consortia place on production, dissemination, and consumption?
4. What consortia do you participate in, and is this voluntary participation? Why participate?

Cryptography

Cryptography (as opposed to steganography, the practice of hiding easily read messages) dates to about 1500 BCE, about 68,000 years after the earliest text in this book. The etymology of the word *cryptography* gives us a pair of words: "secret writing." An encrypted text can be consumed only by one who knows "the secret" of the writing. Cryptography is secret writing in that it both contains and performs a secret. Encrypted texts are usually functional, administrative, and even factual; the labor of encrypting and decrypting a fictional text is largely pointless. We make exception, in this case, for social forms based on extremely pervasive structures of authority; under the conditions created by these forms, even fictional texts can be perceived by the authority to present a threat to its security and sustenance.

As with censorship, some technologies are better suited for encryption than others, though simple enciphering (such as a substitution code, or Morse code) is possible in every technology. The development of cryptography stems from the same fear as censorship: cryptography assumes that textual transmission is potentially uncontrollable. Where censorship regulates texts to protect an authority, cryptography is used to ensure that a text is protected from another authority.

Consider these questions:

1. Why did it take so long, comparatively, for cryptography to emerge?
2. What social forms, and what larger groupings of social forms, does cryptography assume?
3. What social forms are brought into being by the existence of cryptography?
4. What kinds of cryptography go beyond encryption? What kinds of knowledge problems are entangled with cryptography?
5. What is the opposite of cryptography?
6. Which of the other second-order concepts that we have focused on (e.g., production, transmission, consumption, sedimentation, copyright) might need rethinking when it comes to cryptography?

FURTHER READING

Kahn, David. *The Codebreakers*. New York: Scribner, 1996.

Rosenheim, Shawn James. *The Cryptographic Imagination: Secret Writing from Edgar Poe to the Internet*. Baltimore: Johns Hopkins University Press, 1997.

Singh, Simon. *The Code Book: The Science of Secrecy from Ancient Egypt to Quantum Cryptography*. New York: Random House Digital, 2011.

PART 2   HISTORICAL FRAMEWORK

PART 2 FOCUSES ON THE HISTORY of text technologies; the many manifestations, over time, of textual forms; and the ways in which technologies are currently developing. We provide numerous case studies of individual representative artifacts, tools, and textual phenomena, each with a small set of questions asking you to think about the object or phenomenon in particular ways and some suggested reading. Since many of the technologies under discussion here (e.g., Japanese tsunami markers, tablet technology) are either not studied much or are so new that little has been written on them, you should strive to find other articles or books or websites on these textual forms.

Toward the end of this part are more questions for research, together with lists of terms that require your definitions. These sections aim to ensure you have mastered the basics of text technologies and to consolidate the thinking through of the individual items that make up the bulk of this long part of the book.

Additional case studies, many from non-Anglophone traditions, and a number focused on women and gender minorities, can be found at https://texttechnologies.stanford.edu/.

TIMELINES

● *Developments*

▲ *Works*

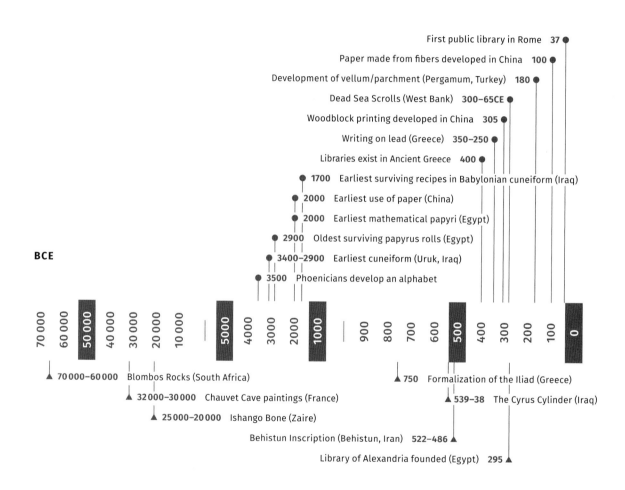

First public library in Rome **37** ●
Paper made from fibers developed in China **100** ●
Development of vellum/parchment (Pergamum, Turkey) **180** ●
Dead Sea Scrolls (West Bank) **300–65CE** ●
Woodblock printing developed in China **305** ●
Writing on lead (Greece) **350–250** ●
Libraries exist in Ancient Greece **400** ●
● **1700** Earliest surviving recipes in Babylonian cuneiform (Iraq)
● **2000** Earliest use of paper (China)
● **2000** Earliest mathematical papyri (Egypt)
● **2900** Oldest surviving papyrus rolls (Egypt)
● **3400–2900** Earliest cuneiform (Uruk, Iraq)
● **3500** Phoenicians develop an alphabet

BCE

70 000 60 000 50 000 40 000 30 000 20 000 10 000   5000 4000 3000 2000 1000   900 800 700 600 500 400 300 200 100 0

▲ **70 000–60 000** Blombos Rocks (South Africa)
▲ **32 000–30 000** Chauvet Cave paintings (France)
▲ **25 000–20 000** Ishango Bone (Zaire)
▲ **750** Formalization of the Iliad (Greece)
▲ **539–38** The Cyrus Cylinder (Iraq)
Behistun Inscription (Behistun, Iran) **522–486** ▲
Library of Alexandria founded (Egypt) **295** ▲

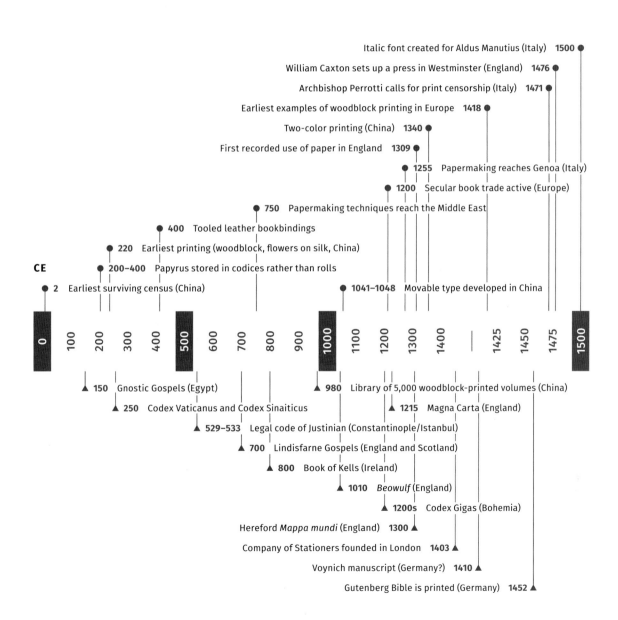

Italic font created for Aldus Manutius (Italy) **1500** ●

William Caxton sets up a press in Westminster (England) **1476** ●

Archbishop Perrotti calls for print censorship (Italy) **1471** ●

Earliest examples of woodblock printing in Europe **1418** ●

Two-color printing (China) **1340** ●

First recorded use of paper in England **1309** ●

● **1255** Papermaking reaches Genoa (Italy)

● **1200** Secular book trade active (Europe)

● **750** Papermaking techniques reach the Middle East

● **400** Tooled leather bookbindings

● **220** Earliest printing (woodblock, flowers on silk, China)

● **200–400** Papyrus stored in codices rather than rolls

CE

● **2** Earliest surviving census (China)

● **1041–1048** Movable type developed in China

0 **100** **200** **300** **400** **500** **600** **700** **800** **900** **1000** **1100** **1200** **1300** **1400** **1425** **1450** **1475** **1500**

▲ **150** Gnostic Gospels (Egypt)

▲ **250** Codex Vaticanus and Codex Sinaiticus

▲ **529–533** Legal code of Justinian (Constantinople/Istanbul)

▲ **700** Lindisfarne Gospels (England and Scotland)

▲ **800** Book of Kells (Ireland)

▲ **980** Library of 5,000 woodblock-printed volumes (China)

▲ **1215** Magna Carta (England)

▲ **1010** *Beowulf* (England)

▲ **1200s** Codex Gigas (Bohemia)

Hereford *Mappa mundi* (England) **1300** ▲

Company of Stationers founded in London **1403** ▲

Voynich manuscript (Germany?) **1410** ▲

Gutenberg Bible is printed (Germany) **1452** ▲

TIMELINES

──────

● *Developments*

▲ *Works*

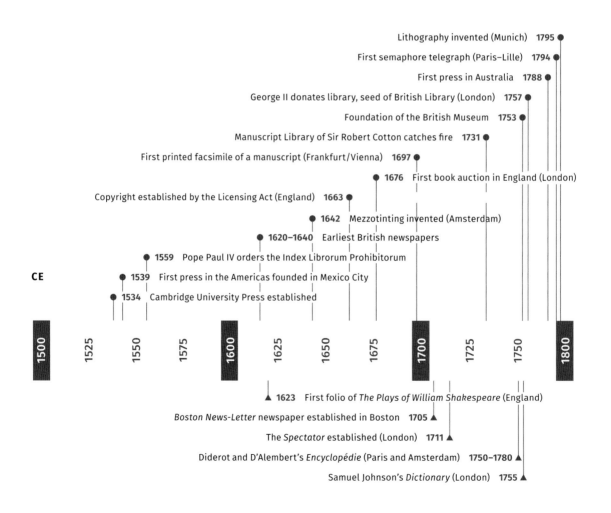

Lithography invented (Munich) **1795** ●

First semaphore telegraph (Paris–Lille) **1794** ●

First press in Australia **1788** ●

George II donates library, seed of British Library (London) **1757** ●

Foundation of the British Museum **1753** ●

Manuscript Library of Sir Robert Cotton catches fire **1731** ●

First printed facsimile of a manuscript (Frankfurt/Vienna) **1697** ●

● **1676** First book auction in England (London)

Copyright established by the Licensing Act (England) **1663** ●

● **1642** Mezzotinting invented (Amsterdam)

● **1620–1640** Earliest British newspapers

● **1559** Pope Paul IV orders the Index Librorum Prohibitorum

CE ● **1539** First press in the Americas founded in Mexico City

● **1534** Cambridge University Press established

1500 1525 1550 1575 **1600** 1625 1650 1675 **1700** 1725 1750 **1800**

▲ **1623** First folio of *The Plays of William Shakespeare* (England)

Boston News-Letter newspaper established in Boston **1705** ▲

The *Spectator* established (London) **1711** ▲

Diderot and D'Alembert's *Encyclopédie* (Paris and Amsterdam) **1750–1780** ▲

Samuel Johnson's *Dictionary* (London) **1755** ▲

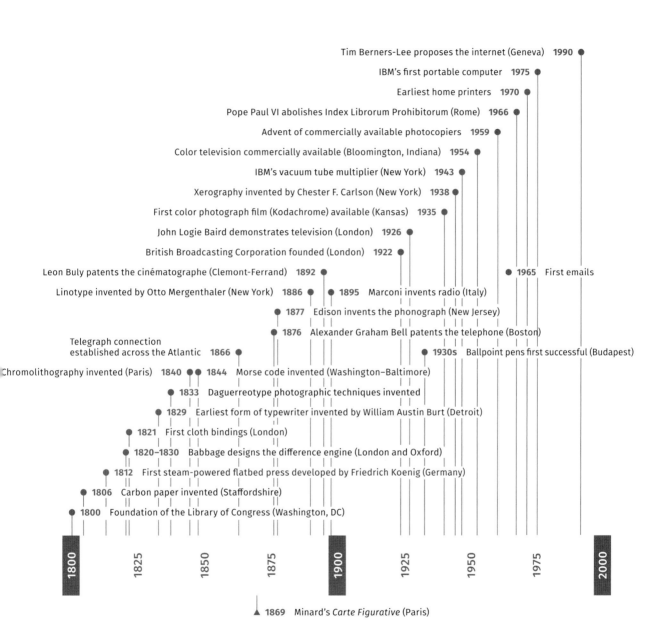

Tim Berners-Lee proposes the internet (Geneva) **1990**

IBM's first portable computer **1975**

Earliest home printers **1970**

Pope Paul VI abolishes Index Librorum Prohibitorum (Rome) **1966**

Advent of commercially available photocopiers **1959**

Color television commercially available (Bloomington, Indiana) **1954**

IBM's vacuum tube multiplier (New York) **1943**

Xerography invented by Chester F. Carlson (New York) **1938**

First color photograph film (Kodachrome) available (Kansas) **1935**

John Logie Baird demonstrates television (London) **1926**

British Broadcasting Corporation founded (London) **1922**

Leon Buly patents the cinématographe (Clemont-Ferrand) **1892**

1965 First emails

Linotype invented by Otto Mergenthaler (New York) **1886**

1895 Marconi invents radio (Italy)

1877 Edison invents the phonograph (New Jersey)

1876 Alexander Graham Bell patents the telephone (Boston)

Telegraph connection established across the Atlantic **1866**

1930s Ballpoint pens first successful (Budapest)

Chromolithography invented (Paris) **1840**

1844 Morse code invented (Washington–Baltimore)

1833 Daguerreotype photographic techniques invented

1829 Earliest form of typewriter invented by William Austin Burt (Detroit)

1821 First cloth bindings (London)

1820–1830 Babbage designs the difference engine (London and Oxford)

1812 First steam-powered flatbed press developed by Friedrich Koenig (Germany)

1806 Carbon paper invented (Staffordshire)

1800 Foundation of the Library of Congress (Washington, DC)

1800 **1825** **1850** **1875** **1900** **1925** **1950** **1975** **2000**

1869 Minard's *Carte Figurative* (Paris)

HISTORICAL TECHNOLOGIES

Writing on Stone

Chauvet Cave Paintings

FURTHER READING

Abadia, Oscar Moro, and Manuel R. Morales Gonzalez. "Thinking about 'Style' in the 'Post-Stylistic Era': Reconstructing the Stylistic Context of Chauvet." *Oxford Journal of Archaeology* 26 (2007): 109–25.

Clottes, Jean. "Chauvet Cave (ca. 30,000 B.C.)." In *Heilbrunn Timeline of Art History*. New York: Metropolitan Museum of Art, 2002. http://bit .ly/195Qqzp.

Pettitt, Paul, Paul Bahn, and C. Züchner. "The Chauvet Conundrum: Are Claims for the 'Birthplace of Art' Premature?" In *An Enquiring Mind: Studies in Honor of Alexander Marshack*, edited by Paul G. Bahn. Oxford: Oxbow Books, 2009.

Snow, Dean. "Sexual Dimorphism in European Upper Paleolithic Cave Art." *American Antiquity* 78 (2013): 746–61.

The Chauvet Cave paintings were discovered by three speleologists in 1994 in Pont-d'Arc, in the Ardèche region of France (see the link to the website in the Figure 1 caption). Estimated to be about 30,000 years old, the paintings, engravings, and drawings contain images of horses, bison, owls, rhinos, and lions, with some additional stylized panels. The cave system extends beyond 1,300 meters and can be compared to the Lascaux caves and other major European prehistoric sites. The paintings make use of the cave wall to create shadow and a three-dimensional effect, which is why Werner Herzog filmed *Cave of Dreams* (2010) in 3D. It is thought that the paint, made from natural pigments, was applied using moss or hair mats, and some appears to have been applied by blowing through a straw. It has been surmised, too, that handprints painted onto the walls may belong to female artists.

QUESTIONS

1. What was the function of these caves?
2. What is the significance of this early form of text?
3. What tools and substrate are employed here? What are the particular characteristics of each?
4. Why might the artists have chosen to create these paintings in these caves?
5. What do these possible choices reveal about the artists and their conception of TEXT?

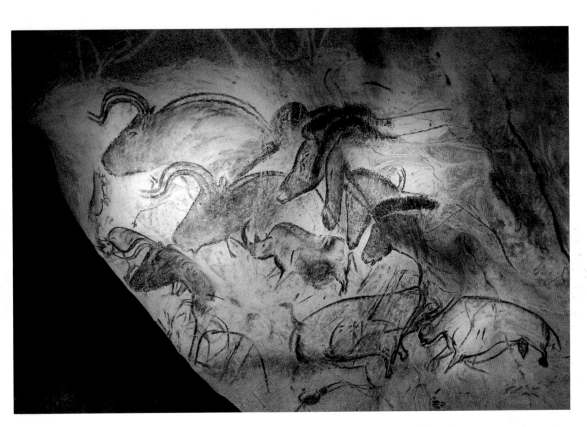

Figure 1
The Chauvet Caves.
Thirty thousand BCE.

Figure 2
Babylonian cuneiform tablet: a
receipt for grain from 2056 BCE in
Sumerian script.

Courtesy Department of Special
Collections, Stanford Libraries.

Babylonian Clay Tablets

There are over 100,000 surviving Babylonian tablets from the period 3400 BCE to perhaps the first century CE (Figure 2). These represent the earliest interpretable writing system in the world. The Sumerian, Babylonian, Assyrian, and Hittite cultures used this form of recording texts. The tablets are made from clay, incised with cuneiform ("wedge shaped": from the Latin *cuneus*, wedge) inscriptions written with a stylus while the clay was moist. Then the clay was baked, making the artifact very durable. A vast array of administrative, legal, mercantile, and commercial information is contained on the tablets, which range in size from an inch to many feet in length and breadth.[1] These tablets also range significantly in shape. Some of the tablets are cushion shaped, some are cylindrical, and some conical. It has taken numerous scholars a great deal of time to translate the varieties of cuneiform, since the interpretation of the symbols is immensely problematic. Great works of literature, like *The Epic of Gilgamesh*, were also made permanent through their inscription onto tablets.

The earliest cuneiforms were pictograms; later, a phonographic element was added.[2] Though the earliest Sumerian cuneiform numbered only 640 characters, the addition of phonograms made the language modular and gave it an effectively infinite number of terms.

FURTHER READING

Glassner, Jean-Jacques. *The Invention of Cuneiform: Writing in Sumer*, translated by Zainab Bahrani and Marc Van De Mieroop. Baltimore: Johns Hopkins University Press, 2003.

Robson, Eleanor. "The Clay Tablet Book in Sumer, Assyria, and Babylonia." In *Blackwell Companion to the History of the Book*, edited by Simon Eliot and Jonathan Rose. Oxford: Wiley-Blackwell, 2008.

On *Gilgamesh*: http://bit.ly/19St4jR.

On the Hammurabi Law Code: http://bit.ly/19gVwfS.

QUESTIONS

1. What kind of language is Sumerian?
2. What are the advantages and disadvantages of this kind of method of textual production?
3. Why might these tablets have been developed? What motivates such innovation?
4. How accessible is this technology to the society it records? What does that imply about its social function?

Figure 3
The Cyrus Cylinder. Sixth century
BCE.

The Cyrus Cylinder

The Cyrus Cylinder (Figure 3) dates from 539 to 538 BCE. Written in cuneiform in Akkadian, it gives an account of the lineage and therefore the legitimacy of King Cyrus, who reigned from 539 to 530 BCE. Cyrus describes how he conquered Babylon with the help of Marduk, the god of Babylon. Cyrus describes the improvements he made to Babylon, having conquered it, and the sacrifices he offered in thanks to Marduk, and declares toleration for worshippers of other religions.

The Cyrus Cylinder is held by the British Museum, and a replica is housed in the United Nations building in New York City. It is widely regarded as an early charter of human rights. Read and critique the translated transcription at http://bit.ly/2dDzACa.

FURTHER READING

Baghoolizadeh, Bheeta. "Reconstructing a Persian Past: Contemporary Uses and Misuses of the Cyrus Cylinder in Iranian Nationalist Discourse." AjamMC.com. http://bit.ly/14uchSZ.

Beaulieu, Paul-Alain. "An Episode in the Fall of Babylon to the Persians." *Journal of Near Eastern Studies* 52 (1993): 241–61.

Finkel, I. L., and M. J. Seymour, eds. *Babylon*. Oxford: Oxford University Press, 2009.

QUESTIONS

1. What is the role of authority in this text? Whose authority is the most important?

2. Why was this text created on a cylinder? It would have been technologically simpler to have it created on a tablet. So what is the import of the text's cylindrical form?

3. Is the Cyrus Cylinder propaganda? If so, for whom?

4. Why might the cylinder of Nabonidus be less well known, even though it is larger, older, and better preserved?

FURTHER READING

Bagnall, Roger S. *The Florida Ostraka:*
Documents from the Roman Army
in Upper Egypt. Durham, NC: Duke
University Press, 1976.
———. *Hellenistic and Roman Egypt:*
Sources and Approaches. Aldershot,
UK: Ashgate, 2006.
Martin, Henri-Jean. *The History and*
Power of Writing, translated by
L. G. Cochrane. Chicago: University
of Chicago Press, 1995.
On the Vindolanda tablets: http://bit.ly
/16uVMnzl.

The Florida Ostraka

Florida State University's Special Collections contains a remarkable and rare collection of thirty-two Roman *ostraka* (sing. *ostrakon*; Ancient Greek, ὄστρακον: meaning earthen vessel, potsherd, hard shell usually inscribed,). This collection comprises letters written by members of a particular unit of the Roman army in the eastern desert of Egypt. Some of these letters are private and informal, and some public and official. Most of the ostraka are written in Greek, though three are in Latin, and all of them are fragments now. One is not genuine. They are datable by close analysis of the names and the script to the period 125 to 175 CE.

Shown here are Bagnall's 21 and 7 as Figures 4 and 5.[3] Figure 4 is written in Greek, and although a good deal of the text is lost on the left, the letter concerns a request for the purchase of fodder and a request for supplies. The writer tells the recipient in line 8 that he cannot go out because he has been ill, but he mentions river travel at line 10. Figure 5 is also written in Greek, and most of the text on the left has been lost. Bagnall states (p. 47): "From the few surviving phrases an air of crisis emerges: the author (perhaps a decurion) has received a letter on ostrakon from Bassos the curator [the commander]; he then questioned the elders (of a village?), and they replied something about having died of famine; the author asks Bassus for precision" (47).

These fragments of a pot, written on in ink, can be compared to the late first- and early second-century Vindolanda tablets, found just south of Hadrian's Wall in the north of England in 1973. These letters are written in ink on thin, postcard-sized sheets of wood (1 mm thick), which were folded after writing; the ink was made from carbon, gum arabic, and water. Until these tablets were discovered, most finds of this kind had been wooden tablets, covered with wax, and written on with a stylus (see http://bit.ly/185s8Vdl).

Figures 4 & 5
An ostrakon—a fragment of a letter in Greek from the second century CE.

Sources: Ostraka 18 (IID) & Ostraka 11, courtesy of Special Collections & Archives, Florida State University Libraries.

QUESTIONS

1. What types of substrate were available to individual writers in these early centuries?

2. What kinds of tools were required to write on these substrates?

3. What are the reasons behind the variety of substrate used, and what are the advantages and disadvantages of each type of material?

Figure 6

The Behistun monument, showing King Darius the Great with the subjugated nations parading before him. Sixth century BCE.

Behistun Monument

Figure 6 shows the remarkable Behistun monument, which is carved into a mountain, 1,700 feet high, in modern Iran. It has been visible to travelers since ca. 520 BCE, when Darius, king of the Persians, defeated his enemies and commemorated those victories in this inscription and sculpture. The monument, engraved at a height of 300 feet, comprises four major elements: (1) a relief sculpture of Darius subduing rebellious subjects; (2) a cuneiform text in Old Persian relating the narrative of conquest; (3) an inscribed text in Babylonian relating the same story as element 2; and (4) the same text inscribed in Elamite (the official language of the Persian Empire). This trilingual text, with its concomitant illustrative relief, suggests that Darius wanted to be sure everybody could

understand the magnificence of his victories. Its position along the Silk Road ensured the success of this public monument and the permanence of Darius's record.

QUESTIONS

1. From linguistic and historical perspectives, what is significant about the Behistun monument?

2. This is a very public inscription that is visible from afar. What role does spatial positioning have in the dissemination of a national monument like this?

3. What prompted the creation of this text, and what impetus might have been behind the specific choice of media?

FURTHER READING

Breasted, J. H. *Ancient Times: A History of the Early World*. Boston: Ginn, 1916. (*Ancient Times* is available at https://archive.org/details/ancienttimeshist00brea.)

Tuplin, C. "Darius' Accession in (the) Media." In *Writing and Ancient Near Eastern Society: Papers in Honour of Alan R. Millard*, edited by Piotr Bienkowski, Christopher Mee, and Elizabeth Slater, 217–44. New York: T&T Clark, 2005.

Figures 7–9
The Rosetta Stone. Second
century BCE.

The Rosetta Stone

The Rosetta Stone (Figures 7–9) was discovered by Captain François-Xavier Bouchard, an officer in Napoleon's army during the Egyptian campaign in 1799. It was found in the wall of the ancient Nile city of Rosetta, and its significance was immediately obvious. It dates from 196 BCE and was made in Egypt; it now resides in the British Museum. Now missing about half of its original mass, the stone is a slab of black granite, measuring 45 by 28.5 by 11 inches, on which is inscribed a text in two languages and three scripts—Egyptian hieroglyphs, demotic (native) Egyptian, and Ancient Greek—of a decree founding a cult of the new king, Ptolemy V. The stone was fundamental in providing information about the meaning of hieroglyphs, when it was translated by Jean-François Champollion in 1822. The last sentence of the inscription reads: "This decree shall be inscribed on a stele of hard stone in sacred [i.e., hieroglyphic] and native [i.e., demotic] and Greek characters and set up in each of the first, second and third temples beside the image of the ever-living king." That one of the three versions of the same text was in Greek, which was read and understood, allowed scholars access to translate, for the first time, the same text in hieroglyphs. In Figure 8, hieroglyphs are seen at the top, demotic Egyptian in the middle, and Greek at the bottom.

FURTHER READING

Andrews, Carol. *The Rosetta Stone.* London: British Museum Press, 1981.

Parkinson, Richard. *Cracking Codes: The Rosetta Stone and Decipherment.* Cambridge: Cambridge University Press, 1999.

Veronis, Jean, ed. *Parallel Text Processing: Alignment and Use of Translation Corpora.* Dordrecht: Kluwer, 2000.

QUESTIONS

1. What is the significance of the size and substrate of the Rosetta Stone?
2. The Behistun inscription and the Rosetta Stone are both public inscriptions. What are the major differences between them? What can you deduce about the differences between the social formations under Ptolemy V and Darius?
3. What is the purpose of the Rosetta Stone's multilingual textuality?

Roman Inscription

The Roman Empire (ca. 40 BCE–410 CE) is one of the greatest civilizations known to humankind. The Romans' inventions were not surpassed for many hundreds of years and included aqueducts, viaducts, central heating, roads, and stone-built engineering. Among the most significant contributions are the Roman alphabet and the Latin language, from which many Western languages—French, Italian, Spanish,

Portuguese—are directly derived. The Roman alphabet is based on Greek (see the Florida Ostraka entry), and it was quickly used for every conceivable form of communication, including public monuments. Epigraphers—scholars of ancient inscriptions—have many rich sources to draw on, with Roman inscriptions being found on thousands of surviving Roman structures. Major scripts used for carving include those known as the Roman square capital and rustic capital, forms of writing developed especially for ease in carving, with angular elements or with limited curvilinear components. Roman capital in particular, is notable for its imperial connotations, and it was used in high-status manuscripts and printed books, as well as on stone and other substrates. Figure 10 shows the highly elaborate carvings on the Arch of Constantine (315 CE), commemorating a military victory by Constantine. Figure 11 shows carved stones being reused in other, later structures, which speaks to how commonplace the practice was, and Figure 12 shows a fragment from the fourth century manuscript known as the Vergilius Augusteus codex, kept at the Vatican Library. Seven leaves from the original manuscript are extant, all written in Roman square capitals (*Capitalis Quadrata* script), a form of writing that deliberately emulated the carved letter-forms of epigraphy. This form of writing is ideologically resonant, reminding readers of the Roman imperial origins of the book, and, indeed of its author, Virgil, who wrote the *Georgics* and *Aeneid*, represented on the surviving leaves.

FURTHER READING

Cooley, Alison E. *The Cambridge Manual of Latin Epigraphy*. Cambridge: Cambridge University Press, 2012.

Goody, Jack. *The Logic of Writing and the Organization of Society*. Cambridge: Cambridge University Press, 1988.

Keppie, Lawrence. *Understanding Roman Inscriptions*. Baltimore: Johns Hopkins University Press, 1991.

Petrucci, Armando. *Public Lettering: Script, Power, and Culture*. Chicago: University of Chicago Press, 1993.

Powell, Barry B. *Writing: Theory and History of the Technology of Civilization*. Oxford, UK: Blackwell, 2009.

Susini, G. C. *The Roman Stonecutter: An Introduction to Latin Epigraphy*, translated by A. M. Dabrowski. Oxford, UK: Blackwell, 1973.

Thomas, Charles. *And Shall These Mute Stones Speak? Post-Roman Inscriptions in Western Britain*. Cardif, UK: Cardiff University Press, 1994.

QUESTIONS

1. How did Latin become so widely known and used?
2. What kinds of tools are used in epigraphy?
3. What limitations are there to epigraphic technology?
4. What are the ideological connotations of the public monument within a city context? What are the most durable of the Roman texts? How does this relate to question 1?
5. How do modern cities use public monuments as TEXT?

Figure 13
Japanese tsunami stone, Aneyoshi.
Twentieth century.

Japanese Tsunami Stones

Ancient tsunami stone monuments dot the northeast coast of Japan, warning of the need to pay attention to the dangers of tsunamis when building homes and settlements. These stone markers are between 4 and 10 feet high. Some are so old that their text is illegible, but the one in Figure 13 from Aneyoshi, which is 4 feet high, reads in translation: "A house on high ground will lead to peace and happiness for posterity. Remember the calamity of the great tsunami. Never build houses from this point down. . . . No matter how many years pass, keep vigilance high." These markers are up to 600 years old, though the one here is about 100 years old (possibly replacing an older stone). The waves from the 2011 tsunami reached 300 feet below this stone, showing that those who heeded the advice of their ancestors could indeed be kept safe.

FURTHER READING

Kohlstedt, Katl. "Tsunami Stones: Ancient Japanese Markers Warn Builders of High Water." August 15, 2016. http://99percentinvisible.org /article/tsunami-stones-ancient -japanese-markers-warn-builders -high-water/.

Lewis, Danny. "Tsunami Stones." *Smithsonian*, August 31, 2015. http:// www.smithsonianmag.com /smart-news/century-old-warnings -against-tsunamis-dot-japans -coastline-180956448/.

QUESTIONS

1. In what ways might one classify these stones, and what parallels can you make with similar forms of communication from other cultures?

2. What are the respective roles of authority and dissemination in these texts?

3. From what sort of social forms does this textual object spring, and what social forms of communication does it envisage for the future?

Figure 14
Breamore church doorway.
Eleventh century CE.

Source: Elaine Treharne.

Breamore Church

Breamore Church in Hampshire, constructed from stone in the late tenth century and altered in later centuries, is one of the most famous churches from Anglo-Saxon England. Of great note within the church is a phrase, written in Old English using legal language, carved into the stones of the arch of the doorway in the south porticus, near the crossing of the church (see Figure 14). The inscription reads: HER SWUTELAÐ SEO GECWYDRÆDNES ÐE (Here, the covenant is revealed to you). This probably refers to Genesis 9:8–17, where God promises Noah never to flood the earth again. At verses 12 and 13, the text reads, "And God said: This is the sign of the covenant which I give between me and you, and to every living soul that is with you, for perpetual generations. I will set my bow in the clouds, and it shall be the sign of a covenant between me, and between the earth."

Carved in Roman square capitals, with Insular Anglo-Saxon runic characters Ð (eth, a "th" sound) and Æ (ash, an "e" sound), this deep inscription is painted with red ochre to make the letters stand out. The arch of the doorway reflects in its shape the rainbow promised in Genesis.

FURTHER READING

Blair, John. "Breamore." In *Blackwell Encyclopaedia of Anglo-Saxon England*, edited by Michael Lapidge, John Blair, Simon Keynes, and Donald Scragg. Oxford, UK: Blackwell, 1999.

Du Boulay-Hill, A. "A Saxon Church at Breamore, Hants." *Archaeological Journal* 55 (1898): 84–87.

Gameson, Fiona, and Richard Gameson. "The Anglo-Saxon Inscription at St Mary's Church, Breamore, Hampshire." *Anglo-Saxon Studies in Archaeology and History* 6 (1993): 1–10.

Okasha, Elizabeth. "English Language in the Eleventh Century: Evidence from Inscriptions." In *England in the Eleventh Century*, edited by Carola Hicks. Stamford, UK: Paul Watkins, 1992.

QUESTIONS

1. What experience does this text seek to create for its audience?
2. What kinds of authority does this text leverage?
3. How does this text aim to be transformative?
4. Can you think of an analogous inscription that you have seen? What effect did it have on you?

Signs

Signs like those in Figures 15 and 16 are so much a part of everyday life that we don't consciously realize what we are seeing, even though we register the instructions or information that the signs communicate. There are incalculable numbers of signs in modern society, taking all manner of forms: the billboard alongside the interstate; the STOP sign at a junction; the large sign or logo indicating a shop's premises; a warning sign on a truck; hazard signs in buildings; a digital sign on a major road warning of traffic hazards; brightly lit signs in a town center; a person dressed as a slice of pizza waving a discount notice. These forms of public writing are significant and ubiquitous, and they have specific intentionalities. Materially, they are very varied, and each is aimed at a different audience.

FURTHER READING

Mehta, V. *The Street: A Quintessential Social Public Space*. London: Routledge, 2013.

Signage Foundation. "Consumer Foundations of Retail Signage." Accessed November 24, 2016, at http://www.signresearch.org/wp-content/uploads/Consumer-Perceptions-in-Retail-Signage-Executive-Summary.pdf.

QUESTIONS

1. What are we calling "public writing" so far? What sorts of authority have we been assuming constitute publicness?
2. What sorts of visual and verbal rhetoric does public signage manipulate?
3. How durable is a text like a STOP sign? Why is it made the way it is?
4. For whom are these texts made? What is the relationship between intentionality and functionality that they aim to ensure?
5. In what ways do businesses seek to ensure that consumers know where their premises are?

Figure 17 (top left)
Graffiti, New York. Twentieth century.

Figure 18 (top right)
Graffiti on church monument. It reads "Singe praises unto the lord O ye saintes of his, 1581 'In te domine speravi non confundar in eternum' G. R." (Psalm 30:2). Sixteenth century CE.

Source: Elaine Treharne.

Figure 19 (right)
Graffiti. Twentieth century.

Graffiti

Graffiti (from Italian *graffito*, a scratch) is a drawing or writing scratched on a wall or other surface. Early graffiti exists from centuries ago, including evidence in ancient towns like Pompeii and Herculaneum, destroyed and petrified by Vesuvius in 79 CE and hidden until 1749. Graffiti can be found throughout history, including deeply engraved graffiti in medieval and early modern churches and castles, with names, initials, symbols, and messages carved into any available surface, from permanent and time-consuming incisions on medieval tombs to scratches in glass. Inscriptions carved into rocks and trees demonstrate that all surfaces are viewed as potential substrates for permanent or long-lasting messages. Other graffiti, such as chalk messages in schools and on university campuses, is often permitted and quickly washed away. Ephemeral graffiti also comes in the form of skywriting, and laser, light, or electronic graffiti projected onto the sides of buildings.

Modern graffiti is most often taken to mean painted, drawn, or sprayed images and words found on the sides of trains. Some graffiti is so stylized in its lettering that it becomes a "forma" script, meaning that, just as in cuneiform script, words can be devised from shapes. Famous examples are documented from the New York subway in the 1980s, and everyday graffiti is found on buildings, bridges, walls, and all manner of other places (Figures 17–19). Graffiti is now often illegal, and there are organizations set up to counter it, report it, and clean it up. Graffiti uses an extraordinary range of substrates and tools and can have almost any intention. It often self-consciously alludes to and manipulates the concept of authority. These factors make graffiti an extraordinarily complex text technology.

QUESTIONS

1. What kinds of classifications of graffiti are possible?
2. What are the tools and substrates most commonly associated with graffiti?
3. What differentiates graffiti from public signage?
4. Why is graffiti vilified by bodies with claims to authority? Is graffiti threatening to you?
5. Why is there controversy over whether graffiti can be art? What are the differences between graffiti and street art?
6. Why do brands try to affiliate themselves with graffiti artists?

FURTHER READING

Austin, Joe. *Taking the Train: How Graffiti Art Became an Urban Crisis in New York City*. New York: Columbia University Press, 2002.

Bowen, Tracey E. "Graffiti Art: A Contemporary Study of Toronto Artists." *Studies in Art Education* 41 (1999): 22–39.

Champion, Matthew. *Medieval Graffiti: The Lost Voices of England's Churches*. London: EBury Press, 2015.

Hermer, Joe, and Alan Hunt. "Official Graffiti of the Everyday." *Law and Society Review* 30 (1996): 455–80.

Kramer, Ronald. "Painting with Permission: Legal Graffiti in New York City." *Ethnography* 11 (2010): 235–53.

Sliwa, Martyna, and George Cairns. "Exploring Narratives and Antenarratives of Graffiti Artists: Beyond Dichotomies of Commitment and Detachment." *Culture and Organization* 13 (2007): 73–82.

Ancient Graffiti Project: http://ancientgraffiti.wlu.edu/hgp/.

Banksy, the British graffiti artist: http://www.banksy.co.uk/.

Street Art and Urban Creativity, a journal: http://www.urbancreativity.org/.

Writing on Cellulose

Papyrus

FURTHER READING

Baikie, James. *Egyptian Papyri and Papyrus-Hunting.* New York: Kessinger, 1926.

Lewis, Naphtali. *Papyrus in Classical Antiquity.* Oxford: Oxford University Press, 1974.

Parkinson, Richard, and Stephen Quirke. *Papyrus.* London: British Museum, 1995.

Roemer, Cornelia. "The Papyrus Roll in Egypt, Greece, and Rome." In *A Companion to the History of the Book,* edited by Simon Eliot and Jonathan Rose, 85–94. Oxford: Wiley-Blackwell, 2009.

Vandendorpe, Christian. *From Papyrus to Hypertext: Toward the Universal Digital Library.* Translated by P. Aronoff and H. Scott. Chicago: University of Illinois Press, 2009.

Making papyrus: http://www.ehow.com /how_4881594_make-egyptian -papyrus.html.

Papyrus manufacture: http://www.lib .umich.edu/papyrus_making/#.

Figure 20 shows a papyrus fragment in the collection at Stanford University Libraries. Papyrus is the origin of the modern word *paper*. It was used for writing from about 3000 BCE to 1000 CE, and it can still be bought today, since its manufacture was rediscovered in the twentieth century. Papyrus is a resilient substrate made from the triangular reedlike stems of the papyrus plant, which grows along the banks of the Nile, but it was also cultivated on plantations in ancient Egypt. The reeds were cut, peeled, cut into strips, soaked, pounded, pressed, dried, polished (with shells or pumice stone), and cut into sheets for writing. Papyrus became the most widely used material in the classical world for writing that was intended to be permanent and stored, and it was exported throughout the Mediterranean. Individual sheets of papyrus are often found, and early copies of the Bible were written on papyrus. It was most used for writing on single sheets or for the formation of rolls of papyrus sheets glued together. Some of these could be very long—many as long as 20 feet.

Books in the first few centuries of the Common Era were also manufactured using papyrus for folios or for strengthening the structure of the volume. Among the former are the famous Nag Hammadi codices discovered in large earthenware pots in northern Egypt in the 1940s. These twelve volumes contain early Christian writings in the Coptic language, dating from the third and fourth centuries. Although Latin, Greek, and other writing systems were frequently used for writing on papyrus, the usual association is with Egyptian hieroglyphics, demotic Egyptian, and Greek.

Writing was done using a brush (in the case of Egyptian scribes, particularly) or a reed pen with a split nib. The black ink of these early writings was usually made of carbon, water, and gum arabic (or acacia gum).

Figure 20
Early papyrus, recycled as the wrapping for an Egyptian mummy (here in the shape of a foot). Second century BCE.

Source: Courtesy Department of Special Collections, Stanford Libraries.

QUESTIONS

1. What made papyrus such a successful substrate?

2. What kinds of writing was papyrus used for? What tools were required?

3. What are the drawbacks of using papyrus for textual production?

4. What writing systems are hieroglyphs? What is demotic script, and for what kinds of text was it most commonly used?

Figure 21 (right)
Early paper (note chain lines and
laid lines, ruling, and sewing holes).
Fifteenth century CE.

Source: Courtesy Department of Special
Collections, Stanford Libraries.

Figure 22 (below)
Watermark on early handmade
paper. Fifteenth century CE.

Source: Courtesy Department of Special
Collections, Stanford Libraries.

Paper

Paper has been around in the West for only about a thousand years, but in China, it has been used since perhaps 100 BCE. Paper can be made from almost any cellulose material. Originally it was made by hand from natural plant fibers such as mulberry and hemp, though this was often coarse and uneven in quality. Once papermaking reached southern Europe, it was made by hand from linen or cotton rags.

Paper takes days to make, but many sheets of paper can be made from one vat, and it is cheaper than producing parchment. In the later medieval West, clean waste linen and cotton were collected by the ragman and brought to paper mills, where the rags were soaked and pulped in a vat. In this process, a mold and deckle—a wire screen in a frame, sometimes with a wire watermark incorporated into the screen—is drawn through the slurry and gently shaken until the pulp forms a flat layer of pulp and liquid. The mold is pressed between felt and drained, and the damp sheets are hung up until they are dry. The sheets are then sized and burnished to ensure a smooth writing surface. Lines visible in the paper from the mold are known as chain (side-to-side) and laid (top-to-bottom) lines (both are visible in Figure 21 but only the laid lines in Figure 22).

In the eighteenth century, machines were invented that made possible the production of paper in large quantities. The Fourdrinier machine, developed at the beginning of the nineteenth century, facilitated the rapid manufacture of paper, though the quality of machine-made paper is never as good as handmade paper.

FURTHER READING

Bloom, Jonathan. *Paper before Print: The History and Impact of Paper in the Islamic World*. New Haven, CT: Yale University Press, 2001.

Cropper, Mark. *The Leaves We Write On: James Cropper; A History in Paper-Making*. London: Ellergreen Press, 2004.

Febvre, Henri, and Henri-Jean Martin. *The Coming of the Book: The Impact of Printing, 1450–1800*. London: Verso, 1997.

Hunter, Dard. *Papermaking: The History and Technique of an Ancient Craft*. New York: Dover, 1978.

Brief overview of papermaking: http://bit.ly/135ZxkD.

QUESTIONS

1. What are the principal characteristics of paper?
2. Why did paper eventually replace parchment (skin or membrane) as the main substrate for writing?
3. When was the process for machine-made paper invented, and what were its major disadvantages in the earliest decades of production?
4. What kinds of text technological innovation might the use of paper have encouraged?

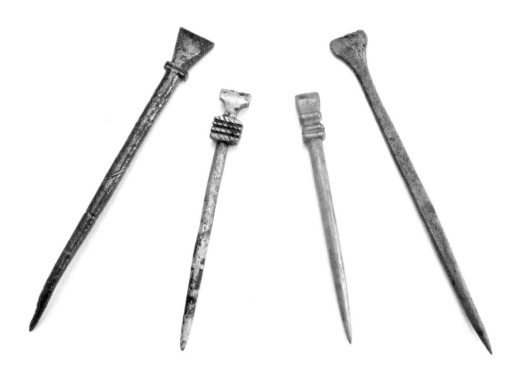

Figure 23 (above)
Medieval styli.

Source: Four examples of medieval styluses, by Numisantica, is licensed under CC BY-SA 3.0 nl. https://en.wikipedia.org/wiki/Stylus#/media/File:Stylus.jpg.

Figure 24 (right)
Wax tablets with stylus.
Twentieth-century replica.

Source: Wax tablet and a Roman stylus, by Peter van der Sluijs, is licensed under CC BY-SA 3.0. https://en.wikipedia.org/wiki/Stylus#/media/File:Table_with_wax_and_stylus_Roman_times.jpg.File:Stylus.jpg.

Wax Tablets

Tablets of wood, bone, metal, slate, or ivory into which a recess was carved formed the basis of wax tablets (Latin: *pugillares* or *tabulas*). These were used by the Egyptians, then throughout the classical and medieval periods up to about 1500, and even later in some places. Beeswax was poured into the recess and could be used for engraving with a stylus—a metal, wood, or bone implement with a point at one end and a spatula at the other, used for erasing (Figure 23). The wax (which could be of various colors, such as black, yellow, red, or green) was re-formed by melting it at 122°F (to create a clean slate, or tabula rasa), and the tablets were then reused for writing new texts. A pair of boards could be laced together, functioning like the opening of a book—a diptych (Figure 24). It was also possible to link multiple boards into a codex form—a polyptych.

The small slate board and chalk that schoolchildren used in the nineteenth century can be seen as the successor to the wax tablet, which itself was employed in teaching students throughout its history. Tablets were used for composing notes, making lists, general administration, and drafts of texts to be copied, among many other kinds of ephemeral writings. Many were lightweight and could be carried like a notebook for rapid recording of information.

FURTHER READING

Bowman, A. K., J. M. Brady, R. S. O. Tomlin, and J. D. Thomas. "A Corpus of Writing-Tablets from Roman Britain." N.d. http://www.csad.ox.ac.uk/rib/ribiv/jp1.htm.

Brown, Michelle P. "The Role of the Wax Tablet in Medieval Literacy: A Reconsideration in Light of a Recent Find in York." *British Library Journal* 20 (1994): 1–17.

Clanchy, M. T. *From Memory to Written Record, 1066–1307*, 3rd ed. Oxford, UK: Wiley-Blackwell, 2012.

Eliot, Simon, and Jonathan Rose, eds. *Companion to the History of the Book*. Oxford, UK: Wiley-Blackwell, 2009.

Szirmai, J. A. "Wooden Writing Tablets and the Birth of the Codex." *Gazette du livre médiéval* 17 (1990): 31–32.

Making wax tablets: http://bit.ly/1czHHcE.

On tablets: http://bit.ly/1exuI85.

Using tablets: http://bit.ly/17CdC5l.

QUESTIONS

1. What kinds of functions might wax tablets be used for?
2. What are the advantages and disadvantages of the form?
3. What has the form of the tablet developed into? What was the inspiration for using this word for modern tablets?
4. Find references to wax tablets in Eliot and Rose's *Companion to the History of the Book*. Why might this significant text technology attract so little scholarly commentary?
5. Why did wax tablets not persist as a substrate?

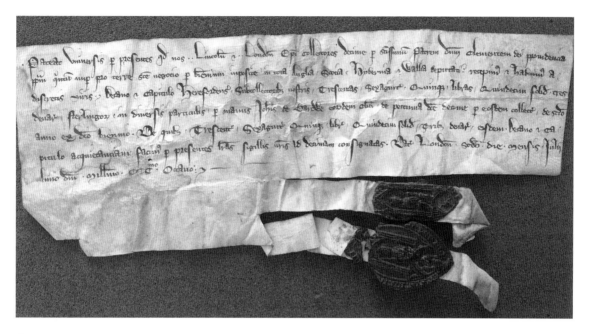

Seals

Seals (the study of which is called sigillography) date back to at least the cuneiform period (3000 BCE–450 BCE), and perhaps the precuneiform. As cylinders in ancient Mesopotamia, seals were rolled onto clay to give a repeating image. As a category, seals include the incised tablets used in early Chinese literary culture to impress a mark of ownership onto a document, which subsequently developed into an art form. In western Europe, imprinted wax impressions were affixed to the bottom of legal or administrative documents, initially by the use of silk or hemp chords or fixed directly onto the document. In many cases, thumbprints are still visible on the reverse of the seal, perhaps as an additional method of authentication.

A seal comprises two parts: a seal matrix or die in metal, stone, bone, or ivory, which is engraved with a design particular to a person or institution, together with the impressions formed from pressing the die onto a malleable and soft surface that hardens (these can include wax or lead). Seals also include the engraved rings still worn today and other relief markings on official letterheads from government, administrative, or educational institutions. Seals can also be used to maintain the integrity of a closed box or container or as a means of identification.

Figure 25 shows an example of a personal seal affixed to a document. Documents issued by the monarchy included much larger royal seals, which were immensely complex and expensive products, and letters sealed, letters patent, and letters imprinted are all so called because of their methods of sealing: respectively, closed by seal; open, with a seal appended; and authenticated with the imprint of a seal.

QUESTIONS

1. What technological niche does a royal seal fill? How does the royal seal have continuity with its Mesopotamian forebear?

2. What are the key textual goals of a seal other than its technological goals? How are those textual goals manifested?

3. Letters were sealed with wax and then imprinted with a ring seal. What aspect of text technology does this use of seals address?

4. What does it mean today to wear a signet ring? Why would you advertise your adherence to a sedimented technology like this?

5. Where in your daily life do you rely on seals? What are their most contemporary equivalents?

FURTHER READING

Collon, Dominique, ed. *7000 Years of Seals*. London: Trustees of the British Museum, 1997.

Harvey, P. D. A., and Andrew McGuinness. *A Guide to British Medieval Seals*. London: British Library and Public Record Office, 1996.

McDermott, Joseph P. *A Social History of the Chinese Book: Books and Literati Culture in Late Imperial China*. Hong Kong: Hong Kong University Press, 2006.

New, Elizabeth A. *Seals and Sealing Practices: Archives and the Users*. London: British Records Association, 2010.

Oikonomidès, Nicolas. *Byzantine Lead Seals*. Washington, DC: Dumbarton Oaks, 1985.

Schofield, Philipp, Sue Johns, Elizabeth New, and John McEwan. "Seals in Medieval Wales." N.d. http://www.aber.ac.uk/en/history/research-projects/seals/.

Introduction to sigillography: http://www.grandricci.org/paraitre_sceaux_leaflet.pdf.

Writing on Animal Skin

Parchment and Vellum

Figure 26 shows a manuscript written on animal membrane or skin, commonly labeled parchment. The image includes a repair to the membrane, where the stitches in the dried and treated animal skin have fallen out. Parchment, named after the city where it was first manufactured (Pergamum, on the coast of present-day Turkey), has been used as a substrate since at least the third century BCE, and possibly some centuries earlier. A shortage of papyrus had led to the search for an alternative substrate, and animal skins were found to be a perfect medium. They are composed of collagen, as opposed to cellulose, and many of the features of animal skin are attractive for bookmakers (its elasticity, its resilience, its ability to be erased and reused and, in some cases, palimpsested, where writing is scraped off and overwritten). Membrane was widely used for making books and documents until the sixteenth century and continues in use today for some kinds of legal documents and bespoke products, made for special occasions. It is still produced by a handful of specialists, principally within the North American market by R. E. Meyer and Sons' company, Pergamena, in Montgomery, New York. For specialists and scholars, "parchment" is often taken to refer to the skin of sheep and "vellum" is used to refer to calfskin. Books and scrolls with membrane folios are also manufactured using deerskin and goatskin.

Membrane requires a particular method of production to make it a successful writing surface. The animal's skin is dipped into vats of a lime solution to depilate the hair and rot the remaining flesh. After soaking for a few days, the skin is thoroughly rinsed, draped over a stand, and scraped with a lunellum (a half-moon-shaped knife). While still wet, the sheet is pegged onto a frame and stretched to its maximum extent. When dry and thus tautly pegged, it is scraped further to remove all traces of flesh and hair, and when done especially expertly, the parchmenter, for whom this is intensely physical work, can scrape down to the channel of the vein. When the surface is smooth, the parchment is cut into a large rectangle and then cut and folded into sheets of the appropriate size for book or document production. This process is time-consuming and expensive, and no book written on membrane is likely to be cheaply or easily produced.

FURTHER READING

Avrin, L. *Scribes, Script and Books.* London: British Library, 1991.

Brown, Michelle. "The Triumph of the Codex: The Manuscript Book before 1100." In *Companion to the History of the Book,* edited by Simon Eliot and Jonathan Rose, 179–93. Oxford, UK: Wiley-Blackwell, 2009.

Clanchy, M. T. *From Memory to Written Record, 1066–1307,* 3rd ed. Oxford, UK: Wiley-Blackwell, 2012.

———. "Parchment and Paper: Manuscript Culture 1100–1500." In *Companion to the History of the Book,* edited by Simon Eliot and Jonathan Rose, 194–206. Oxford, UK: Wiley-Blackwell, 2009.

Clemens, Ray, and Timothy Graham. *An Introduction to Manuscript Studies.* Ithaca, NY: Cornell University Press, 2007.

Parkes, M. B. *Their Hands before Our Eyes: A Closer Look at Scribes.* London: Routledge, 2008.

Watch Jesse Meyer make parchment in the first part of this video: http://bit .ly/13LLaQX/.

J. Paul Getty Museum, "Making Parchment": http://bit.ly/15Uapjp/.

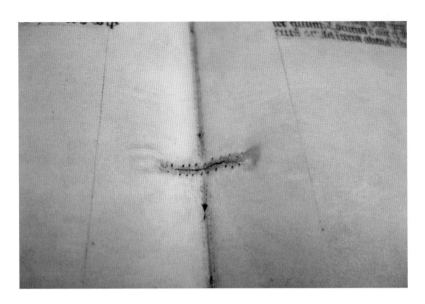

Figure 26
Membrane prepared for medieval
manuscript. Fifteenth century CE.

Source: Elaine Treharne.

The finest vellum is bright white and very thin and flexible. It is made from young calfskin, or even the skin of stillborn calves, which is immensely expensive. Membrane can also be quite thick and suede-like, and when the resource is particularly scarce or in great demand, the horny end pieces of the prepared skin or other waste pieces are sometimes used in the preparation of books or documents. Skin that has holes or other flaws is frequently seen in the production of medieval books too; the holes were often caused by a knife nick during preparation, and these are frequently repaired today through stitching. Scars from ticks or other injuries sustained by the animal in life are also visible in manuscripts, and these, together with DNA analyses, are providing scholars with significant evidence about this major text technological resource and its uses in the classical and medieval world.

QUESTIONS

1. Why was membrane such a widely adopted substrate? What are its major text technological attributes?

2. Watch and make brief notes on the two videos listed in "Further Reading."

3. What would you use membrane for now? Is all contemporary membrane to be considered a sedimented technology? What technological edge does membrane retain as a substrate?

Figure 27

Hereford *mappa mundi*. Interactive images of the Hereford *mappa mundi* are available at https://commons.wikimedia.org/wiki
/File:Mappa_mundi_Hereford_1300_explained.png.

The Hereford *Mappa Mundi*

A *mappa mundi* was a common genre of map in medieval Europe, and numerous examples, ranging from simplified diagrams to fully illustrated representations of the known world, are found in manuscripts from 500 CE to 1500 CE. The example in Figure 27, now housed at Hereford Cathedral, is a single-leaf document and is the largest and best preserved of these maps, dating to the late thirteenth century. The map's substrate is a single piece of vellum. The map's configuration depicts the profoundly theological psychogeography of the time: Jerusalem is shown as the center of the world, and east is at the top (hence the word *orientation*, with its etymology from *oriens*, east). The map also records the varied flora, fauna, and peoples of the world according to the latest research at the time. This includes sea monsters and other "known" monsters of the world. England and Scotland are shown at the bottom left of the map.

QUESTIONS

1. What does the substrate declare about text? What sizes of vellum are we used to seeing?

2. What sorts of resources were necessary to create the Hereford map? What might this text have been used for?

3. How does this map differ from a map that you might buy to take on a road trip or differ again from an online map? What other textual functions are combined into the Hereford *mappa mundi*?

FURTHER READING

Foys, Martin, and Shannon Bradshaw. "Developing Digital Mappaemuni: An Agile Mode for Annotating Medieval Maps." *Digital Medievalist* 7 (2011). http://www.digitalmedievalist.org /journal/7/foys/.

Harley, J. B. *The History of Cartography*, vol. 1. Chicago: University of Chicago Press, 1992.

Harvey, P. D. A. *Mappa Mundi: The Hereford World Map.* London: British Library Studies in Medieval Culture, 1996.

Hereford *mappa mundi* in 3D: http:// www.themappamundi.co.uk/explore .php.

Figure 28
Medieval scroll. Thirteenth century CE.

Source: Courtesy Department of Special Collections, Stanford Libraries.

The Scroll

A scroll is a roll of membrane, papyrus, or paper, usually with writing on it. Papyrus is usually rolled, since it becomes brittle if folded, and thus papyrus and the scroll represent a perfect combination of material and form. A scroll is an ancient technology and has been used for writing since at least the third millennium BCE. A scroll can be one rolled-up sheet or sheets sewn or glued together. Writing usually occurs on only one side of the scroll, which must be unrolled in order to access specific parts of the text. Some of the most famous examples of the scroll form are the Dead Sea Scrolls, the first of which were found in caves in Qumran in 1947. In Judaism, the Torah is found in scroll form. The oldest currently known Judaic scroll dates to ca. 800 CE. The scroll in Figures 28 and 29, made of multiple sheets of calfskin sewn together using strips of vellum, outlines a legal case in Italy in the later Middle Ages. In medieval England, most of the administrative work of the Exchequer and the royal courts was recorded on membrane rolls (sometimes a roll is considered a shorter version of a scroll). In Japanese art, the makimono is a scroll painting on silk. Some Chinese scroll books are made from narrow strips of bamboo, which are then sewn onto a silk backing and stored in rolled-up format. Scrolls are often stored in boxes (*capsa*) or within textile covers horizontally on shelves.

QUESTIONS

1. What are the advantages and disadvantages of the scroll format in comparison with the codex (see the next entry)?
2. What are the Dead Sea Scrolls, and why are they important?
3. What has modern technology derived from this older form of textual production?
4. What can you deduce about a culture whose founding text was written on a scroll and which kept that technology? How are that culture and that text technology interwoven?

Figure 29
Scroll close-up.

Source: Courtesy Department of Special
Collections, Stanford Libraries.

FURTHER READING

Roberts, C. H., and T. C. Skeat. *The Birth
of the Codex*. London: Oxford
University Press, 1983.

Suarez, Michael, and Henry R.
Woodhuysen. *The Oxford
Companion to the Book*. Oxford:
Oxford University Press, 2010.

Writing the Torah: http://bit.ly/1czl334.

On accessing information within scrolls:
http://bbc.in/1982Y9B.

Figure 30 (left)
Medieval manuscript, Stanford
University Library, Codex M501.
Thirteenth century CE.

Source: Courtesy Department of Special
Collections, Stanford Libraries.

Figure 31 (right)
Medieval manuscript, Cambridge
University Library, Gg. 1.1. Early
fourteenth century CE.

Source: Courtesy of Digging Deeper
Project, Stanford University.

The Codex

The codex as a form probably began in about the second century CE,
though there is some earlier evidence of it. The wide dissemination of
the codex was facilitated by its adoption as the principal textual means
of information within the early Christian church. As Christianity spread
throughout western Europe, it made a prolific success of the codex. Indeed, the codex is probably the most significant form in the history of
literate cultures, and it has new life in the twenty-first century through
the e-book, blook, and other digitized forms. We are present-day wit-
nesses of and participants in the most significant technological moment
since printing was made known in Europe in the fifteenth century: as
we work on the codex as a text technology, apocalypticists insist its demise is imminent, while artists and collectors focus on a return to the
book as artifact. Interest in rare books, antiquarian books, and artists'
books seems to be very much on the increase.

The codex is most often composed of folios, leaves, or (when counted
as single sides) pages of membrane or paper, folded into gatherings
(quires), which are usually sewn down the middle, before being sewn to
one another to form the text block (see Figure 30). In turn, this block is
sewn into, or slipped inside, a binding, which acts to protect the interior
of the codex. Bindings can often be highly elaborate and are manufactured
from a wide range of materials. In the Middle Ages, "hardcover" books
had boards of oak covered in leather or cloth; "softcover" books were
limp-bound using parchment or vellum, or chemises, which are covers
made from jackets of softened membrane or cloth.

Many other kinds of books exist beyond the codex that is familiar in the Western tradition. These range from Chinese bamboo books to Tamil palm-leaf books and accordion books. Artists' books deliberately play with the form to test its potential and exploit all elements of "bookness" (see Figure 31). Books appear ubiquitously in artistic culture and have particular symbolism in different contexts: the depiction of a book in a painting, for example, might indicate scholarship and wisdom or manifest the presence of spiritual inspiration of some kind, and memorials or tombstones are often sculpted as book-shaped.

QUESTIONS

1. What genres of text are contained within the earliest codices? What texts are contained in their modern equivalents?

2. Find five different contexts in which books appear as symbols.

3. What do the following terms mean: folios, bifolia, and quires?

4. What are the strengths and limitations of the form of the book?

5. What sorts of texts are likely to be contained in the book? What conception of the individual, and of the relationship between individual and society, does the book presume?

FURTHER READING

Carrière, Jean-Claude, and Umberto Eco. *This Is Not the End of the Book: A Conversation Curated by Jean-Philippe de Tonnac*. London: Vintage, 2012.

Cave, Roderick, and Sara Ayad. *A History of the Book in 100 Books*. London: British Library, 2014.

Chartier, Roger. *The Order of Books*. Stanford, CA: Stanford University Press, 1994.

Johns, Adrian. *The Nature of the Book: Print and Knowledge in the Making*. Chicago: University of Chicago Press, 2000.

Lyons, Martyn. *Books: A Living History*. London: Thames and Hudson, 2013.

Martin, Henri-Jean. *The History and Power of Writing*. Chicago: University Chicago Press, 1988.

Price, Leah. *How to Do Things with Books in Victorian England*. Princeton, NJ: Princeton University Press, 2012.

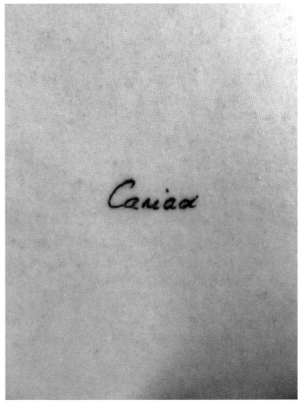

Figure 32 (left)
Twentieth-century tattoos.

Source: Courtesy of Henk Schiffmacher.

Figure 33 (right)
Tattoo saying "Cariad" (Darling).
Twenty-first century.

Source: Courtesy of Sioned Hughes.

Tattoos

Skin is a flexible and portable substrate, and any kind of skin is suitable for writing or inscribing (Figures 32 and 33). In terms of human skin, the earliest recorded tattoos are prehistoric. These include tattoos inscribed on acupuncture points on the body of Ötzi the Iceman (a mummy datable to ca. 5400 BCE, who was found in 1991 in the Italian Alps).

Tattoos take a number of forms and are done using a variety of techniques, with different effects. Modern Western tattoos are done by needle and ink and are inspired by the tattoo culture of native Polynesian tribes. The tradition of Polynesian tattoos (*tatau*), including those of the Maori in New Zealand, goes back over two thousand years and is specialized and symbolic—a sacred rite. Masters of the tattoo process are regarded as cultural remembrancers, and they control who can and cannot have a tattoo within the tribal structure. The master (*kahuna* in Hawai'i) marks out the design and then taps the skin with sharp needles made of bone or turtle shell, for example, which are attached to a wooden haft. Soot from burned candlenut mixed with oil or sap produces the ink. In Japan, traditional tattoos (*Irezumi*) involve hand-tapping a needle made from bamboo into the skin. In some cultures, tattoos are associated with the criminal underworld, and the whole process of tattooing, together with its symbolic meaning, is highly secretive and considered subversive.

A notable project involving tattooing, *Skin*, was designed and composed by Shelley Jackson (http:// ineradicablestain.com/skin.html). In this project, individual participants were sent a single word that they were to have tattooed onto their body. All of these individuals combined created a literary work, fragmented by their geographically disparate whereabouts. As each "word" dies, so the literary work—never effected as a whole—will dissipate entirely. This is a fascinating artistic use of the technology.

QUESTIONS

1. What might motivate an individual to get a tattoo?
2. What functions do tattoos serve?
3. What different kinds of tattooing techniques can you find?
4. What is the creative impetus behind *Skin*, and why have people signed up to participate?
5. Think about the interplay that tattooing relies on between body as living organism and living body as legible substrate. What kind of interplay of production, authority, and dissemination does this posit? Why do you think that tattooing is increasingly popular? What do you think the future possibilities of tattooing might be with the development of implant technologies and electronic ink?

FURTHER READING

Caplan, Jane, ed. *Written on the Body: The Tattoo in European and American History*. Princeton, NJ: Princeton University Press, 2000.

Jackson, Shelley. "Skin." 2003–10. http:// ineradicablestain.com/skin.html.

Newman, Simon P. "Reading the Bodies of Early American Seafarers." *William and Mary Quarterly* 55 (1998): 59–82.

Olguin, B. V. "Tattoos, Abjection and the Political Unconscious." *Cultural Critique* 27 (1996): 159–213.

Sanders, Clinton R. *Customizing the Body: The Art and Culture of Tattooing*. Philadelphia: Temple University Press, 1989.

van Dinter, Maarten Hesselt. *The World of Tattoo: An Illustrated History*. Amsterdam: KIT Publishers, 2005.

Earliest tattoos: http://bit.ly/15e7xKp.

Ötzi the Iceman: http://bit.ly/18cI08g.

FORM AND FUNCTION

Manuscript Culture

Manuscript culture extends from the earliest periods of writing to the present day. Two examples from the fifteenth century and the nineteenth, are shown in Figures 34 and 35. Every time someone picks up a writing implement, say, a pen or a brush, the resulting writing or inscription is manuscript (Latin: *manuscriptus—manus + scribere*—handwritten). Another term for *manuscript* is *chirograph* (Greek, *chiro + graph*, written by hand). This technology is thousands of years old and is manifested in a multitude of forms, though we most commonly think of books, booklets, and single leaves as manuscripts.

Manuscript culture is deeply imbued with uniqueness: no manuscript can be identical to any other, even if the layout and text are meant to be the same. Handwriting changes dramatically according to the nature of the text or the rhetoric of the page. A personal letter looks quite different from a page of a large Bible, even if those texts have been written by the same scribe. Moreover, the copying out of the same text by a single scribe will contain differences that can vary in scale from the alteration of words and phrases, to the inclusion of errors, spelling, and punctuation variation and inconsistent capitalization and abbreviation. This is called textual mouvance and concerns the variants between copies of the same text.

The majority of medieval scribes and artists were highly trained individuals, though linguistic competence was not guaranteed. Scribes learned to write to particular models of writing, called script, until the twentieth century. In some cultures, the most proficient scribal work is still carried out by professional scribes, some of whom have a spiritual role in the culture to which they belong. The tools of the scribe varied according to the tradition in which he or she wrote (and writes even to this day).

FURTHER READING

Brantley, Jessica. "The Prehistory of the Book." *PMLA* 124 (2009): 632–39.

Brown, Michelle P., and Scott McKendrick, eds. *Illuminating the Book: Makers and Interpreters; Essays in Honour of Janet Backhouse*. London: British Library, 1998.

Brownrigg, Linda L., ed. *Making the Medieval Book: Techniques of Production*. Los Altos Hill, CA: Anderson-Lovelace / Red Gull, 1995.

Da Rold, Orietta. "Materials." In *The Production of Books in England, c.1350–1530*, edited by Alexandra Gillespie and Daniel Wakelin, 12–33. Cambridge: Cambridge University Press, 2011.

Egan, Ron. "To Count Grains of Sand on the Ocean Floor: Changing Perceptions of Books and Learning in Song Dynasty China." In *Knowledge and Text Production in an Age of Print: China, 900–1400*, edited by Lucille Chia and Hilde De Weerdt, 33–62. Leiden: Brill, 2011.

Griffiths, Jeremy, and Derek Pearsall, eds. *Book Production and Publishing in Britain, 1375–1475*. Cambridge: Cambridge University Press, 1989.

Ker, Neil R. *English Manuscripts in the Century after the Norman Conquest*. Oxford, UK: Clarendon Press, 1960.

Love, Harold. *Scribal Publication in Seventeenth-Century England*. Oxford: Oxford University Press, 1993.

Marotti, Arthur F., and Michael D. Bristol. *Print, Manuscript, and Performance: The Changing Relations of the Media in Early Modern England*. Columbus: Ohio University Press, 2000.

Pens and illumination: http://bit.ly /18cHRSu.

Preparation of materials: http://bit .ly/11OhK3i.

The writing of sacred texts: http://bit .ly/11OhMYU.

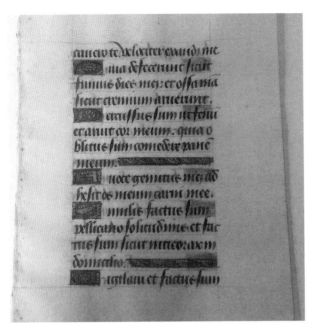

Figure 34
Medieval manuscript leaf from a Book of Hours, France. Fifteenth century CE.

Source: Elaine Treharne.

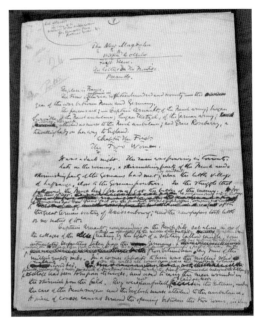

Figure 35
Wilkie Collins's 1871 manuscript of *The New Magdalen*.

Source: Courtesy Department of Special Collections, Stanford Libraries.

QUESTIONS

1. What are the characteristics of any manuscript culture?

2. What tools did a scribe use for medieval manuscript production?

3. Why are manuscripts so highly valued?

4. What manuscripts do you make?

5. Libraries and archives refer to any nonpublished text, whether handwritten or not, as a manuscript. What does this imply about the perceived status of authority and dissemination in a manuscript?

Figure 36
Thirteenth-century Bible (showing
Isaiah 31–32 and 39–40).

A Bible

Figure 36 shows a bifolium, a cut and folded sheet forming a pair of folios, or four pages, for writing. It is from a thirteenth-century Bible that originated in Paris. The text is from the Book of Isaiah from the Latin Vulgate version of the Bible. This was the version of the Bible translated by Saint Jerome (d. 420 CE), which became the standard text in the Western Catholic Church (see http://www.latinvulgate.com/). There are two columns per folio, the writing grid being ruled with a pencil, with an average of seven words per line, written in a formal Gothic bookhand, with a tiny broad-edged quill. This form of codex, with its very small and condensed script, meant that the whole Bible could be copied into one portable volume, common in the thirteenth century and later.

New information retrieval tools began to appear at this time. Chapter numbers are provided in red and blue inks, with some pen-drawn flourishes on the opening words of each chapter, and running heads in red and blue ink also appear at the top of folios from the twelfth century onwards. These function to permit readers easier access to their place in the text. There are also marginal annotations, showing that some readers were highly engaged with the text they were reading. This interaction with manuscripts is common but becomes an expected part of the scholastic endeavor from the middle of the twelfth century. This was chiefly a result of the intellectual enterprise of the newly founded universities across western Europe, which encouraged active intervention as part of an intense reading process.

FURTHER READING

de Hamel, Christopher. *The Book: A History of the Bible*. London: Phaidon Press, 2001.

Smalley, Beryl. *The Study of the Bible in the Middle Ages*, 3rd ed. South Bend, IN: University of Notre Dame Press, 1983.

QUESTIONS

1. For whom might the Bible in Figure 36 have been written?
2. What seems particular to manuscript culture in the example shown here? What features are found here that do not occur in printed books?
3. How might scholars deduce the date of this manuscript?

Figure 37 (above)
French Book of Hours. Binding and
lost contents. ca. 1490.

Source: Elaine Treharne.

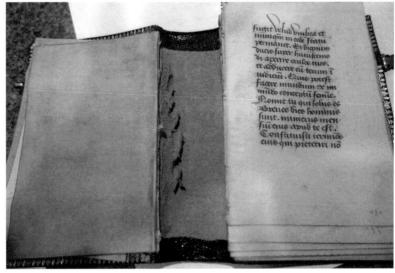

Figure 38 (right)
French Book of Hours. Interior.

Source: Elaine Treharne.

A Book of Hours

Figures 37 and 38 show the remains of a small Book of Hours, a devotional collection of psalms, prayers, and an ecclesiastical calendar for home use, usually based on a shortened version of the hours of prayer in monasteries. It was produced in northern France around 1460. It measures approximately 3.5 by 5 inches, though the leaves have been trimmed for a new clasped binding. These fragments in their nineteenth-century clasped binding were bought in 2013, in the belief that the book had been dismembered decades before, since it was common in the nineteenth and early twentieth centuries to break up medieval manuscripts and sell off individual leaves. Collectors at that time also used to cut up manuscripts and create other objects from them (lamp shades, for example), or simply manufacture scrapbooks from excised illuminated initials, as John Ruskin was in the habit of doing.

It transpires, though, that this book of hours was whole, numbering over 250 pages, when it was sold for about £25,000 by the London auctioneer Christie's. The antiquarian book dealer who purchased the complete Book of Hours and then cut it up sold individual leaves on eBay for many hundreds of dollars each, utterly destroying the integrity of the historical artifact for profit. Books, unlike paintings and other objects, seem not to be considered works of art despite being protected by the UNESCO 1970 Convention on the Illicit Trafficking of Cultural Property, and thus book breaking continues to be a profitable concern for numerous booksellers, especially through online marketplaces.

FURTHER READING

Mauk, Ben. "Scattered Leaves." *New Yorker*, January 6, 2014. http://www .newyorker.com/currency-tag /scattered-leaves.

Treharne, Elaine. "The Broken Book." November 23, 2013. http:// historyoftexttechnologies.blogspot .co.uk/2013/11/the-broken-book-ii -from-book-of-hours.html.

UNESCO Convention on the Illicit Trafficking of Cultural Property. 1970. http://www.unesco.org/new/en /culture/themes/illicit-trafficking -of-cultural-property/1970 -convention/text-of-the -convention/.

QUESTIONS

1. What can the remnants of manuscripts tell us about the probable form of the book when it was first constructed?
2. What are your views on book breaking (biblioclasm)?
3. Look at eBay under "Antiques, Manuscripts" and see if you can detect individual leaves being sold that might have come from broken books. How much do these leaves cost, and what drives their economic value?

Figure 39 (above)
Opening of antiphonal. Fifteenth
century CE.

Source: Courtesy of Special Collections
& Archives, Florida State University
Libraries.

Figure 40 (right)
Antiphonal binding.

Source: Courtesy of Special Collections
& Archives, Florida State University
Libraries.

An Antiphonal

Figures 39 and 40 show an antiphonal, a medieval and Renaissance music book used in Catholic Church services to sing the liturgy. This example, from Florida State University, Strozier Library (SPC M 214 M36 No. 15), measures 26 by 18.5 inches. It might be datable to the fifteenth century, but neumes (the musical notes) are notoriously difficult to date; even the Gothic writing is standard and difficult to pinpoint in terms of date and place. The manuscript is written on skin, probably one whole skin per opening, which makes it a very resource-heavy book. It was, however, essential for the successful completion of divine service. The page in Figure 39 has been carefully ruled with red ink, and initials introducing each prayer and its response are beautifully decorated. These large initials act as information retrieval tools: place markers for the readers of the text. The manuscript's impressive oak and leather binding, kept separately now, measures 29 by 19 inches and weighs a significant amount—perhaps 30 pounds. This large book, designed to be used by a number of people in a public setting, is quite different from the Book of Hours discussed in the previous entry, which is clearly intended for private, devotional use, since it is such a small volume.

FURTHER READING

Brown, Michelle P., and Patricia Lovett. *The Historical Source Book for Scribes.* Toronto: University of Toronto Press, 1999.

Hiley, David. *Western Plainchant: A Handbook.* Oxford: Clarendon Press, 1983.

Kephart, Rick. "Gregorian Chant Notation." http://bit.ly/1ev5rvm.

QUESTIONS

1. Why is the interplay of form and function so significant in the antiphonal?
2. What might the characteristics of this particular manuscript's mode of production reveal about its probable reception?

Figure 41
Voynich manuscript.
Fifteenth century CE.

Source: Cipher Manuscript,
Beinecke Library, MS 408.

Voynich Manuscript

The Voynich manuscript, named for Wilfrid M. Voynich, who bought it in 1912, dates to around 1400 (Figure 41). The manuscript now rests in the Beinecke Rare Book and Manuscripts Library at Yale University. It was bought in 1586 by Holy Roman Emperor Rudolph II for 600 gold ducats, a considerable sum of money.

The Voynich manuscript is thought by some to have been written by Roger Bacon and seems to be a combination of a florilegium (a compilation of excerpts from other writings), an astronomical or astrological handbook, a bestiary, and a pharmacopia. The manuscript is written in a system akin, perhaps, to hieroglyphs that have never been decoded. A currently popular theory holds that the manuscript is in fact a hoax with no coherent legible meaning. Have a look at the manuscript here and decide what you think the codex represents: http://beinecke.library.yale .edu/collections/highlights/voynich-manuscript.

QUESTIONS

1. What kind of text technologies does the Voynich manuscript mobilize?
2. If the Voynich manuscript is a hoax, what kind of text is it? What was it designed to do? What is its attitude toward authority?
3. If the content of the Voynich manuscript is legible (which is a more fertile supposition), why would the text have been encrypted? What are the implicit claims of any encrypted text?
4. Why might we still care what the Voynich manuscript says?

FURTHER READING

Brumbaugh, R. S. *The Most Mysterious Manuscript: The Voynich "Roger Bacon" Cipher Manuscript.* Carbondale: Southern Illinois University Press, 1978.

Clemens, Ray, ed. *The Voynich Manuscript.* New Haven, CT: Yale University Press, 2016.

Goldstone, Lawrence, and Nancy Goldstone. *The Friar and the Cipher: Roger Bacon and the Unsolved Mystery of the Most Unusual Manuscript in the World.* New York: Doubleday, 2005.

Johnson, Reed. "The Unread: The Mystery of the Voynich Manuscript." *New Yorker,* July 9, 2013.

Manly, John Matthews. "Roger Bacon and the Voynich Manuscript." *Speculum* 6 (1931): 345–91.

Montemurro, Marcelo A., and Damián H. Zanette. "Keywords and Co-Occurrence Patterns in the Voynich Manuscript: An Information-Theoretic Analysis." *PLoS One* 8, no. 6 (June 20, 2013), e66344. doi:10.1371 /journal.pone.0066344.

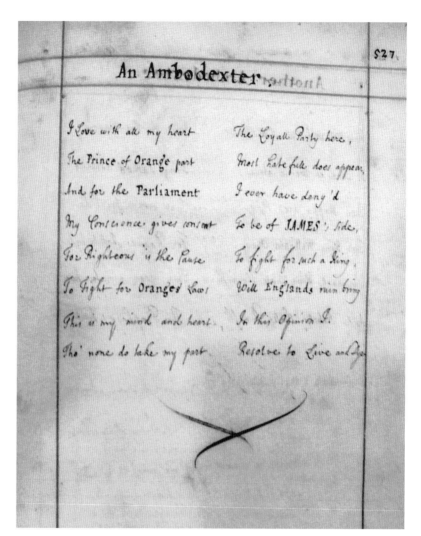

Jacobite Manuscript Poetry

Jacobite poetry was written under adverse political circumstances. Jacobites were Britons who wanted to restore the exiled royal line of the Catholic house of Stuart to the throne of Great Britain between 1688 and 1750 or so. Institutional hostility to their politics was so strong that their beliefs were labeled treasonous. Anyone caught with an identifiably Jacobite piece of writing could be exiled or killed.

Jacobites therefore kept their writing in manuscript, since printing was so cumbersome, and their poems adopted rhetorical tactics that tried to build in some plausible deniability. Some poems were written to be ambiguous, and most played heavily on puns and double meanings. "The Ambodexter" is a poem copied dozens of times after ca. 1684 in manuscripts that were, essentially, private. The poem is generally written in two columns: reading one column at a time makes "The Ambodexter" seem favorable to one side in the English Civil War, whereas when it is read across the two columns, in long lines, it is favorable to the *other* side. This and other poems were written on single sheets of paper, folded up, and passed from hand to hand. If they had to be sent through the post, the recipient would obscure his or her name and address to restore anonymity to the text. These manuscripts now rest in libraries around the world, where they are largely forgotten.

FURTHER READING

Pittock, Murray G. H. *Poetry and Jacobite Politics in Eighteenth-Century Britain and Ireland.* Cambridge: Cambridge University Press, 1994.

Willan, Claude. "Seeing the King over the Water, Two Ways." *English Studies*, August 31, 2017, 1–23. doi:10.1080/001 3838X.2017.1332023.

QUESTIONS

1. Would these poems be the same without the pressure of censorship?
2. What kinds of authority are important in these texts?
3. What is different about the functioning of dissemination in these texts from texts that we have seen so far in this history?
4. Do the strategies employed by Jacobite poets count as cryptography? Why, or why not?

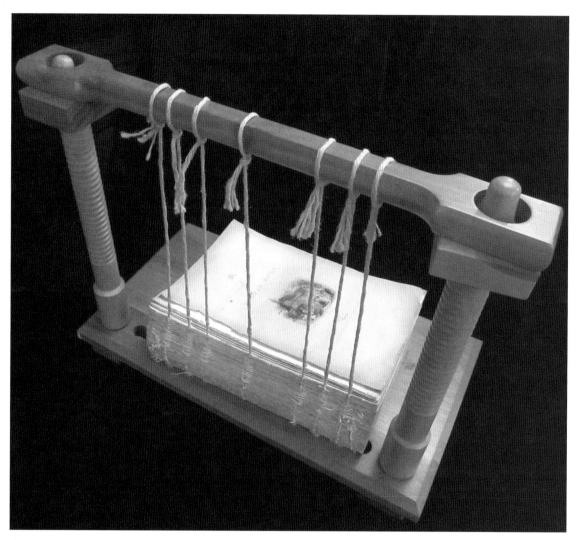

Figure 43
Binding frame. Twentieth century.

Bookbinding

Books are bound in order to ensure that the folios in their quires or gatherings remain intact and to provide protection to ensure the longevity of the contents. Gatherings are sewn down their middle, folded and stacked, and then attached to one another before being bound into the covers of the book. The binding frame in Figure 43 shows the kind of equipment used for binding books in this way. Some forms of bookbinding represent specialist art forms, with oak boards covered in leather or cloth and adorned with decoration ranging from stamping devices to gold plates bejeweled with gemstones. In the early modern period (1500–1800), books could be sold unbound so owners could choose their own bindings. Methods of bookbinding vary around the world. In East Asian practices, for example, stitched binding provides the means for containing the contents of the book. In recent centuries, diverse forms of binding have emerged depending on the cost of the books. These range from paperback books with glued-in contents to ring-bound books.

FURTHER READING

Diehl, Edith. *Bookbinding: Its Background and Technique*. New York: Dover, 1980.

Foot, Mirjam. *The History of Bookbinding as a Mirror of Society*. London: British Library, 1998.

Johnson, Arthur W. *Manual of Bookbinding*. New York: Charles Scribner's Sons, 1978.

QUESTION

1. Look at the binding frame in Figure 43. What can you deduce about bookbinding from the size and shape of the object, in terms of portability, scalability, and the social forms surrounding the early production of books?

Figure 45 (below)
Diamond Sutra. Cave 17, Dunhuang,
ink on paper. Ninth century CE.

Source: British Library. Or.8210/P.2.

Woodcuts and Block Printing

In the early fifteenth century, woodcuts were developed as a technology for producing small images sold either individually (single-leaf woodcut) or used as part of a larger page design. The woodblock is cut in relief, and once ink has been rolled over it, the image is pressed onto paper or membrane, a process also known as xylography. The image shown in Figure 44 is a relatively simple woodcut design illustrating the fourteenth-century saint Bridget of Sweden.

Blockbooks are printed one or two pages at a time from a block of wood that has been carved in relief with text or text and image. The block would be inked up and many individual pages created from that one block. The Diamond Sutra (Figure 45), one of the most famous textual artifacts in the world and now in the British Library, was created in this way in ninth-century China. Buddhist works, written in Chinese, have been printed using xylography on sheets of paper, pasted together to form a long scroll.

In Europe, blockbooks seem to have emerged slightly earlier than printing with movable type, around the mid-fifteenth century. The rapid success of movable type meant that xylography was never particularly prolific as the sole technology for book production, but woodcut images were frequently used as the means of illustration in printed books in the early centuries of print in Europe.

QUESTIONS

1. What are the characteristics of these forms of textual production?
2. What, if any, are the advantages of these forms of print over manuscript?
3. What kinds of texts were produced in the West using xylography?
4. How does xylography most commonly continue in use?

FURTHER READING

Bliss, D. P. *A History of Wood-Engraving*, rev. ed. London: British Museum, 1964.

Hind, A. M. *An Introduction to a History of Woodcut*. New York: Dover, 1935; repr., Boston: Houghton and Mifflin, 1963.

McDermott, Joseph. *A Social History of the Chinese Book*. Hong Kong: Hong Kong University Press, 2006.

Steinberg, S. H. *Five Hundred Years of Printing*, 2nd ed. London: Penguin Books, 1961.

Figure 46
Gutenberg Bible leaf. Fifteenth
century CE.

The Gutenberg Bible

Figure 46 shows a leaf from the Gutenberg Bible. In or around 1450, Johannes Gutenberg (1400–1468), a German inventor, produced the first major work in Europe published using movable type. He had been experimenting with individual page printing for some time prior to 1450, when he invented a wooden-framed printing press and metal type that could be used for large-scale projects like his Bible. The ink he used was particularly black because of its significant metallic component. He produced perhaps as many as 180 Bibles, 145 of them printed on Italian handmade paper, the remainder being printed on vellum. Of these, almost fifty survive in libraries and private collections around the world, and it is one of the most famous books ever produced.

This invention has been widely heralded as one of the most significant of all time, and it initiated what many scholars label the "age of print" and the "print revolution." This text technological transformation in the second half of the fifteenth century and into the sixteenth can be thought of as akin to the major transformation in the way information is provided that is currently underway in our digital age.

FURTHER READING

Childress, Diana. *Johannes Gutenberg and the Printing Press*. Minneapolis: Twenty-First Century Books, 2008.

Eisenstein, Elizabeth L. *The Printing Revolution in Early Modern Europe*, 2nd rev. ed. Cambridge: Cambridge University Press, 2005.

McLuhan, Marshall. *The Gutenberg Galaxy: The Making of Typographic Man*. Toronto: University of Toronto Press, 1962.

On European printing: http://bit.ly/14sqqNO.

On Gutenberg and early print: http://bit.ly/13LMdQI.

QUESTIONS

1. What are the key characteristics of the text technology of printing?

2. Why might the invention and development of printing be thought of as a revolution?

3. Identify some political, religious, and social revolutions that you think printing helped to foster.

4. How does the print revolution differ from the manuscript revolution to which scholars do not usually refer, but which we might well imagine having taken place when substrates and tools for manuscript became widely available?

5. What are the main features of the page layout (also known as the *mise-en-page*) of these early printed books?

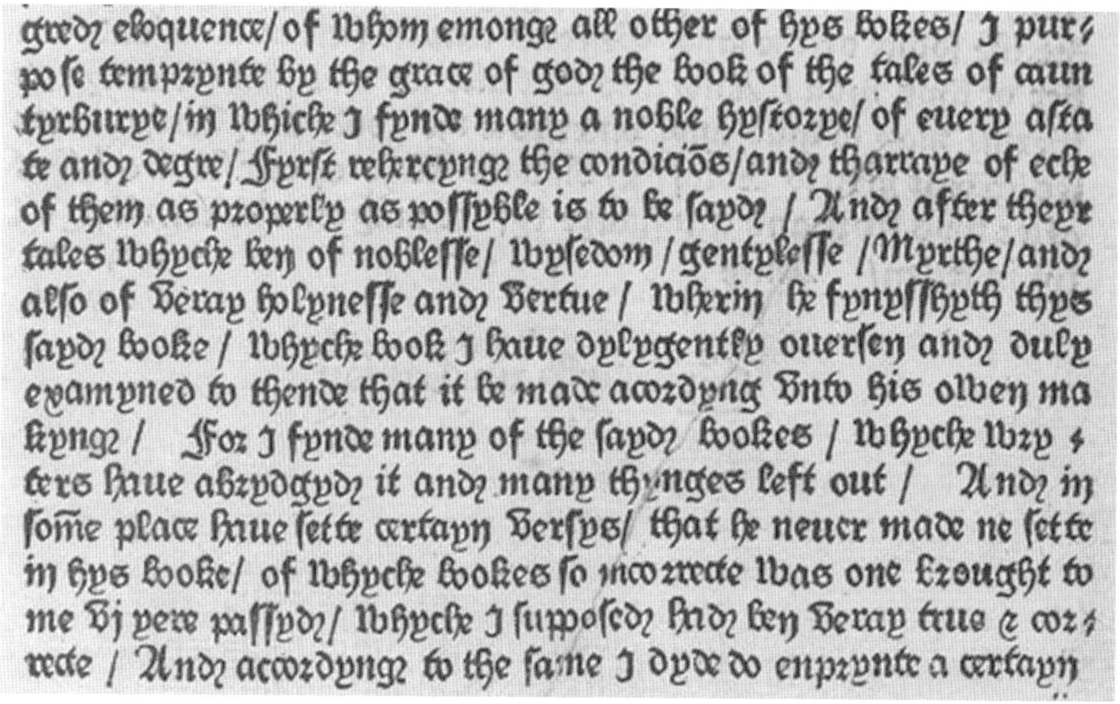

gredz eloquence/of whom emonge all other of hys bokes/ J pur=
pose temprynte by the grace of god the book of the tales of caun
tyrburye/in whiche J fynde many a noble hystorye/ of every asta
te and degre/ Ffyrst rekreynge the condicios/and thartaye of eche
of them as properly as possyble is to be sayd / And after theyr
tales whyche ben of noblesse/ wysedom /gentylesse /Myrthe/and
also of veray holynesse and vertue / wherin he fynysshyth thys
sayd booke / whyche book J have dylygently ouersen and duly
examyned to thende that it be made acordyng vnto his owen ma
kynge / Ffor J fynde many of the sayd bokes / whyche wry =
ters haue abrydgyd it and many thynges left out / And in
some place haue sette certayn versys/ that he neuer made ne sette
in hys booke/ of whyche bokes so incorrecte was one brought to
me vj yere passyd/ whyche J supposed And ben veray true & cor=
recte / And acordyng to the same J dyde do enprynte a certayn

Figure 47
Caxton's *Canterbury Tales*.
Fifteenth century CE.

Source: British Library. G.11586.

William Caxton and Early Modern Printing

Figure 47 is an extract from William Caxton's *Canterbury Tales*. Caxton (1422–91/92) learned about printing when he was on the European Continent, and he brought the first printing press to London in the mid-1480s. He printed a large number of works, most of them in English or French, and thus helped to establish a literary canon. He also contributed to the foundation of a literary standard, particularly in the major vernaculars of England. His work thus had an immeasurable impact on the development of English literature and the professionalization of literary production in particular.

FURTHER READING

Chartier, Roger. *The Order of Books.* Stanford, CA: Stanford University Press, 1994.

Hellinga, Lotte. "The Gutenberg Revolutions." In *A Companion to the History of the Book*, edited by Simon Eliot and Jonathan Rose, 207–19. New York: Wiley-Blackwell, 2007.

Kuskin, William. *Symbolic Caxton: Literary Culture and Print Capitalism.* Notre Dame, IN: University of Notre Dame Press, 2008.

Robinson, Solveig C. *The Book in Society: An Introduction to Print Culture.* London: Broadview, 2013.

QUESTIONS

1. What is the significance of Caxton's work?
2. How did Caxton view his role in textual production?
3. Compare and contrast the images of an early printed book, known as an incunabulum (Figure 46 and 47) and a manuscript page (such as Figure 36). What are the major differences?

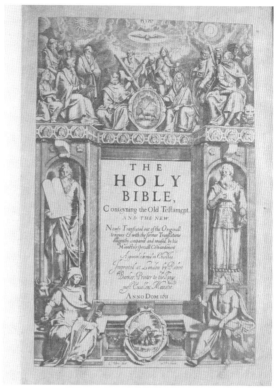

Figure 48
The Great Bible, title page.
Sixteenth century CE.

Figure 49
The King James Bible, title page.
Seventeenth century CE.

Protestant Bibles

The Great Bible (Figure 48) was printed in 1539 and the King James Bible (Figure 49) in 1611. The Great Bible was the first authorized Bible translated into English and was closely associated with King Henry VIII and his efforts, through the work of scholars, like Myles Coverdale, to reform the Anglican Church. The King James Bible, commissioned in 1604 by King James I of England, was a new translation of the Bible into English, completed by a team of scholars in seven years. It has significant status because it has become a textual icon of the English-speaking world. Its impact on the development of English is immensely important; it would have been heard extensively through its use in church services, and as it became more affordable, many families would have owned a King James Bible. Particular phrases in the Bible, such as "salt of the earth," "from strength to strength," and "by the skin of one's teeth," have become embedded within idiomatic English usage.

FURTHER READING

Campbell, Gordon. *The Bible: The Story of the King James Version*. Oxford: Oxford University Press, 2011.

McGrath, Alister. *In the Beginning: The Story of the King James Bible and How It Changed a Nation, a Language and a Culture*. New York: Anchor Books, 2002.

Nicolson, Adam. *Power and Glory: Jacobean England and the Making of the King James Bible*. London: HarperCollins, 2003.

QUESTIONS

1. What is the function of the title page? How does it function as a text in and of itself?

2. What kinds of information do these title pages contain?

3. Look up the phrases "giving up the ghost," "putting words in my mouth," and "by hook or by crook." Which of these are derived from the King James Bible?

Bad Quarto (1603)

Ham. To be,or not to be, I there's the point,
To Die, to ſleepe,is that all? I all:
No,to ſleepe,to dreame, I mary there it goes,
For in that dreame of death, when wee awake,
And borne before an euerlaſting Iudge,
From whence no paſſenger euer retur'nd,
The vndiſcouered country, at whoſe ſight
The happy ſmile,and the accurſed damn'd.
But for this,the ioyfull hope of this,
Whol'd beare the ſcornes and flattery of the world,
Scorned by the right rich,the rich curſſed of the poore?
The widow being oppreſſed,the orphan wrong'd,
The taſte of hunger, or a tirants raigne,
And thouſand more calamities beſides,
To grunt and ſweate vnder this weary life,
When that he may his full *Quietus* make,
With a bare bodkin, who would this indure,
But for a hope of ſomething after death?
Which puſles the braine, and doth confound the ſence
Which makes vs rather beare thoſe euilles we haue,
Than flie to others that we know not of.
I that,O this conſcience makes cowardes of vs all,
Lady in thy orizons, be all my ſinnes remembred.

Good Quarto (1604-1605)

Ham. To be, or not to be, that is the queſtion,
Whether tis nobler in the minde to ſuffer
The ſlings and arrowes of outragious fortune,
Or to take Armes againſt a ſea of troubles,
And by oppoſing, end them, to die to ſleepe
No more, and by a ſleepe, to ſay we end
The hart-ake, and the thouſand naturall ſhocks
That fleſh is heire to; tis a conſumation
Deuoutly to be wiſht to die to ſleepe,
To ſleepe, perchance to dreame, I there's the rub,
For in that ſleepe of death what dreames may come
When we haue ſhuffled off this mortall coyle
Muſt giue vs pauſe, there's the reſpect
That makes calamitie of ſo long life:
For who would beare the whips and ſcornes of time,
Th'oppreſſors wrong, the proude mans contumely,
The pangs of deſpiz'd loue, the lawes delay,
The inſolence of office, and the ſpurnes
That patient merrit of th'vnworthy takes,
When he himſelfe might his quietas make
With a bare bodkin; who would fardels beare,
To grunt and ſweat vnder a wearie life,
But that the dread of ſomething after death,
The vndiſcouer'd country, from whoſe borne
No trauiler returnes, puzzels the will,
And makes vs rather beare thoſe ills we haue,
Then flie to others that we know not of.
Thus conſcience dooes make cowards,
And thus the natiue hiew of reſolution
Is ſickled ore with the pale caſt of thought,
And enterpriſes of great pitch and moment,
With this regard theyr currents turne awry,
And looſe the name of action. Soft you now,
The faire *Ophelia*, Nimph in thy orizons
Be all my ſinnes remembred.

First Folio (1623)

Ham. To be, or not to be, that is the Queſtion:
Whether 'tis Nobler in the minde to ſuffer
The Slings and Arrowes of outragious Fortune,
Or to take Armes againſt a Sea of troubles,
And by oppoſing end them: to dye, to ſleepe
No more; and by a ſleepe, to ſay we end
The Heart-ake, and the thouſand Naturall ſhockes
That Fleſh is heyre too? 'Tis a conſummation
Deuoutly to be wiſh'd. To dye to ſleepe,
To ſleepe, perchance to Dreame; I, there's the rub,
For in that ſleepe of death, what dreames may come,
When we haue ſhufflel'd off this mortall coile,
Muſt giue vs pawſe. There's the reſpect
That makes Calamity of ſo long life:
For who would beare the Whips and Scornes of time,
The Oppreſſors wrong, the poore mans Contumely,
The pangs of diſpriz'd Loue, the Lawes delay,
The inſolence of Office, and the Spurnes
That patient merit of the vnworthy takes,
When he himſelfe might his *Quietus* make
With a bare Bodkin? Who would theſe Fardles beare
To grunt and ſweat vnder a weary life,
But that the dread of ſomething after death,
The vndiſcouered Countrey, from whoſe Borne
No Traueller returnes, Puzels the will,
And makes vs rather beare thoſe illes we haue,
Then flye to others that we know not of.
Thus Conſcience does make Cowards of vs all,
And thus the Natiue hew of Reſolution
Is ſicklied o're, with the pale caſt of Thought,
And enterprizes of great pith and moment,
With this regard their Currants turne away,
And looſe the name of Action. Soft you now,
The faire *Ophelia*? Nimph, in thy Orizons
Be all my ſinnes remembred.

Figure 50
Variant versions of *Hamlet*. 1603.

Source: British Library. C.34.k.1.

Shakespeare's Works

Shakespeare's plays were printed in the sixteenth and seventeenth centuries in a variety of formats. The smaller format, the quarto, was cheaper than the large format, the folio. Folios were prestige editions; quartos were more likely to be reading editions.

Scholars now dispute the authority of different editions, since invariably a slightly (or even very) different text was printed in each different edition. For example, the 1603 edition of *Hamlet* is now known as "the Bad Quarto" and exists in only a small number of copies (Figure 50). It's an action-driven story that scholars think was put together by memorial reconstruction by two actors whose lines were suspiciously well remembered. Mel Gibson's movie *Hamlet* is a production of this text. The second quarto of *Hamlet* dates from 1604/05 and is known as "the Good Quarto." It is much longer, more readerly (since it repays patient reading), and would take about five hours to perform in full. It is much more like Kenneth Branagh's movie *Hamlet*. The text of *Hamlet* in the First Folio of the complete plays in 1623 is somewhere between the two in tone but in places contains yet a third text. These variant versions are digitized in full and discussed in detail on the British Library's website (http://www.bl.uk/treasures/shakespeare/hamlet.html).

Although Ben Jonson was the first to issue a big prestige folio edition of his *Workes* in 1616, Shakespeare's *Complete Works* has proven the more successful and went through many more editions (four by 1685), corresponding to his enduring popularity.

FURTHER READING

Egan, Gabriel. *The Struggle for Shakespeare's Text: Twentieth-Century Editorial Theory and Practice.* Cambridge: Cambridge University Press, 2010.

Holland, Peter, and Stephen Orgel, eds. *From Performance to Print in Shakespeare's England.* New York: Palgrave Macmillan, 2008.

Orgel, Stephen, and Sean Keilan, eds. *Shakespeare and the Editorial Tradition.* New York: Garland, 1999.

QUESTIONS

1. In the images illustrated on the British Library website at its Treasures in Full exhibition (under *Hamlet*), what are the major differences between any two versions of the text?

2. What do these variant editions demonstrate about the nature of early print culture?

3. Can you think of anything that has appeared recently in multiple editions at the same time? What was the reason for that? What does this tell you about the publication history of Shakespeare?

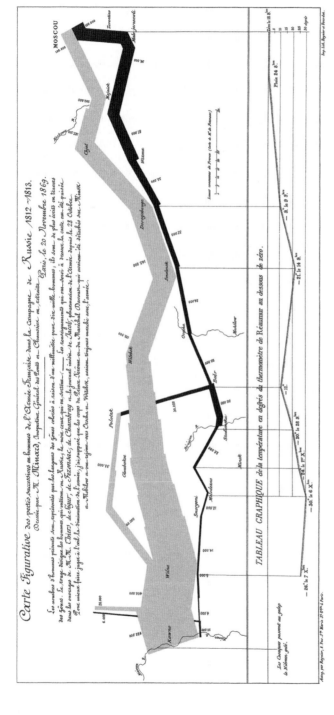

Figure 51

Minard's *Carte Figurative*. 1812.

Lithography

Minard's *Carte Figurative*

French engraver Charles Minard's *Carte Figurative des pertes successives en hommes de l'Armée Française dans la campagne de Russie 1812–1813* dates to 1869 and was one of the last pieces he completed (Figure 51). This image is printed using the lithographic method, invented in the later eighteenth century, where a print was made from a drawing of wax or oil on stone or smooth metal plate (today, polymer images on a thin aluminum plate). Measuring 25½ by 30¾ inches, the *Carte Figurative* represents the emperor Napoleon Bonaparte's disastrous march into and retreat from Russia over the winter of 1812–13. Napoleon set out with 422,000 men and returned with only 10,000. The chart doesn't just show the geographical location of Napoleon's army and its size; it also maps temperature and the direction of travel. It might be one of the most effective pieces of antiwar propaganda ever created.

FURTHER READING

Robinson, Arthur H. "The Thematic Maps of Charles Joseph Minard." *Imago Mundi* 21 (1967): 95–108.

Tufte, Edward. *The Visual Display of Quantitative Information*. Cheshire, CT: Graphics Press, 2001.

Wainer, Edward. "How to Display Data Badly." *American Statistician* 38 (1984): 136–47.

QUESTIONS

1. The *Carte Figurative* conveys a huge amount of information without initially appearing to do so. How does it do that? How many dimensions of information does the text show?

2. How does the text marshal its information into an argument?

3. Think about France's situation in 1869. Why would Minard want to create such a potent antiwar text at this particular moment?

4. What does the existence of a text like this, from a citizen, tell you about the constitution of that citizen's society?

Figure 52
The Illustrated London News. 1865.

Source: Elaine Treharne.

Chromolithography

Chromolithography was a method of creating multicolor prints developed in the 1830s that persisted into the 1930s. It started out as a way of creating original images or replicas of text. As production costs diminished and the process was automated, it became a cheap way to mass-produce images, especially advertisements. Each color to be imprinted on an image would be applied to its own metal or stone plate, so many blocks would be used per single composite image. The *Illustrated London News*, for example, a very popular newspaper, used color for the first time in its 1855 Christmas edition, and advertisements and posters increasingly used color for effect as the nineteenth century progressed (as in Figure 52).

FURTHER READING

Allen, Alistair. *The History of Printed Scraps*. London: New Cavendish Books, 1983.

Glanz, Dawn. "The Democratic Art: Pictures for a Nineteenth-Century America, Chromolithography, 1840–1900 (Review)." *Winterthur Portfolio* 16 (1981): 96–99.

Stankiewicz, Mary Ann. "A Picture Age: Reproductions in Picture Study." *Studies in Art Education* 26 (1985): 86–92.

Twyman, Michael. *A History of Chromolithography: Printed Colour for All*. London: British Library, 2013.

QUESTIONS

1. Color prints were capable of carrying much more information than traditional lithographs. What kind of society would create the demand for texts like chromolithographic reproductions of original art texts?

2. Are chromolithographic reproductions texts in their own right?

3. What tools and substrates could be used in chromolithography?

4. What kind of text would a brand-new chromolithograph be today?

Reading for Everyone

Newspapers

FURTHER READING

Blanchard, Margaret A., ed. *History of the Mass Media in the United States, An Encyclopedia*. London: Routledge, 1998.

Dooley, Brendan. "From Literary Criticism to Systems Theory in Early Modern Journalism History." *Journal of the History of Ideas* 51 (1990): 461–86.

Emery, Michael, Edwin Emery, and Nancy L. Roberts. *The Press and America: An Interpretive History of the Mass Media*, 9th ed. Boston: Allyn and Bacon, 1999.

Espejo, Carmen. "European Communication Networks in the Early Modern Age: A New Framework of Interpretation for the Birth of Journalism." *Media History* 17 (2011): 189–202.

Jefferson, Thomas. "Letters." http://press -pubs.uchicago.edu/founders /documents/amendl_speechs8 .html.

Newspapers began in the early modern period with the production of periodicals reporting the daily news, like the *London Gazette*, which began in 1665 (Figure 53 shows a 1705 edition), and the printing of ephemera like almanacs and chapbooks. The *London Gazette* claims to be the oldest continuous newspaper and is now the official reporter of news for the British government.

Newspapers flourished in a period when there was a notable increase in literacy and much more efficient means of producing them (particularly with mechanization after 1800). In a letter to Virginia statesman Edward Carrington in 1787, Thomas Jefferson declared, "Were it left to me to decide whether we should have a government without newspapers, or newspapers without a government, I should not hesitate a moment to prefer the latter." The significance of the newspaper for the provision of fresh information, reported with some degree of objectivity, was clear. Thousands of local, national, and international newspapers sprang up subsequently, providing billions of readers with their main source of daily or weekly current affairs. Over the previous decade, however, all print newspapers have come under increasing threat from digitally mediated news.

QUESTIONS

1. What is the typical layout of a newspaper? How does form complement function?
2. How do newspapers define what constitutes "news"?
3. Compare mechanisms for the dissemination of news today with those of traditional print-format newspapers. What are the major differences?

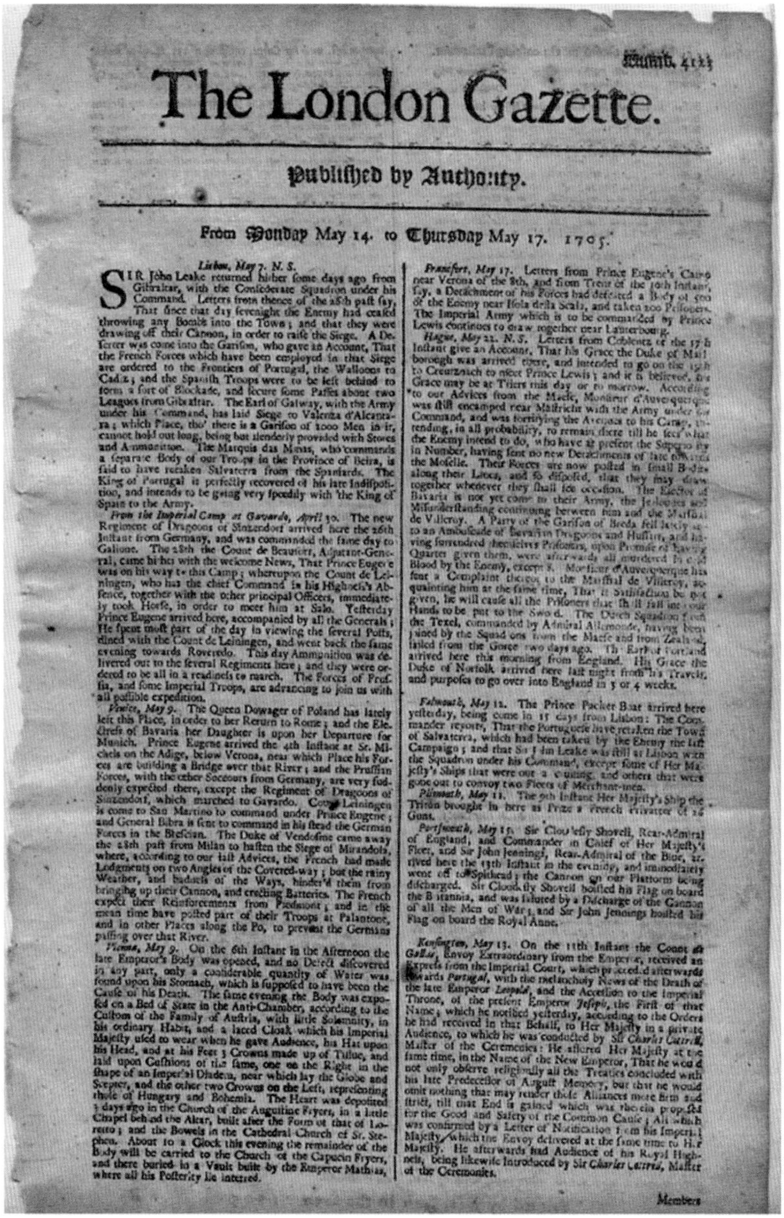

Numb. 4123

The London Gazette.

Publiſhed by Authority.

From Monday May 14. to Thurſday May 17. 1705.

Lisbon, May 7. N. S.

SIR John Leake returned hither ſome days ago from Gibraltar, with the Confederate Squadron under his Command. Letters from thence of the 28th paſt ſay, That ſince that day ſevenight the Enemy had ceaſed throwing any Bombs into the Town; and that they were drawing off their Cannon, in order to raiſe the Siege. A Deſerter was come into the Gariſon, who gave an Account, That the French Forces which have been employed in that Siege are ordered to the Frontiers of Portugal, the Walloons to Cadiz; and the Spaniſh Troops were to be left behind to form a ſort of Blockade, and ſecure ſome Paſſes about two Leagues from Gibraltar. The Earl of Galway, with the Army under his Command, has laid Siege to Valenza d'Alcantara; which Place, tho' there is a Gariſon of 1000 Men in it, cannot hold out long, being but ſlenderly provided with Stores and Ammunition. The Marquis das Minas, who commands a ſeparate Body of our Troops in the Province of Beira, is ſaid to have retaken Salvaterra from the Spaniards. The King of Portugal is perfectly recovered of his late Indiſpoſition, and intends to be going very ſpeedily with the King of Spain to the Army.

From the Imperial Camp at Gavardo, April 30. The new Regiment of Dragoons of Sinzendorf arrived here the 26th Inſtant from Germany, and was commanded the ſame day to Galione. The 28th the Count de Beaufort, Adjutant-General, came hither with the welcome News, That Prince Eugene was on his way to this Camp; whereupon the Count de Leiningen, who has the chief Command in his Highneſs's Abſence, together with the other principal Officers, immediately took Horſe, in order to meet him at Salo. Yeſterday Prince Eugene arrived here, accompanied by all the Generals; He ſpent moſt part of the day in viewing the ſeveral Poſts, dined with the Count de Leiningen, and went back the ſame evening towards Roveredo. This day Ammunition was delivered out to the ſeveral Regiments here; and they were ordered to be all in a readineſs to march. The Forces of Pruſſia, and ſome Imperial Troops, are advancing to join us with all poſſible expedition.

Venice, May 9. The Queen Dowager of Poland has lately left this Place, in order to her Return to Rome; and the Electreſs of Bavaria her Daughter is upon her Departure for Munich. Prince Eugene arrived the 4th Inſtant at St. Michels on the Adige, below Verona, near which Place his Forces are building a Bridge over that River; and the Pruſſian Forces, with the other Succours from Germany, are very ſuddenly expected there, except the Regiment of Dragoons of Sinzendorf, which marched to Gavardo. Count Leiningen is come to San Martino to command under Prince Eugene; and General Bibra is ſent to command in his ſtead the German Forces in the Breſcian. The Duke of Vendoſme came away the 28th paſt from Milan to haſten the Siege of Mirandola, where, according to our laſt Advices, the French had made Lodgments on two Angles of the Covered-way; but the rainy Weather, and badneſs of the Ways, hinder'd them from bringing up their Cannon, and erecting Batteries. The French expect their Reinforcements from Piedmont; and in the mean time have poſted part of their Troops at Palantone, and in other Places along the Po, to prevent the Germans paſſing over that River.

Vienna, May 9. On the 6th Inſtant in the Afternoon the late Emperor's Body was opened, and no Defect diſcovered in any part, only a conſiderable quantity of Water was found upon his Stomach, which is ſuppoſed to have been the Cauſe of his Death. The ſame evening the Body was expoſed on a Bed of State in the Anti-Chamber, according to the Cuſtom of the Family of Auſtria, with little Solemnity, in his ordinary Habit, and a laced Cloak which his Imperial Majeſty uſed to wear when he gave Audience, his Hat upon his Head, and at his Feet 3 Crowns made up of Tiſſue, and laid upon Cuſhions of the ſame, one on the Right in the ſhape of an Imperial Diadem, near which lay the Globe and Scepter, and the other two Crowns on the Left, repreſenting thoſe of Hungary and Bohemia. The Heart was depoſited 3 days ago in the Church of the Auguſtine Fryers, in a little Chapel behind the Altar, built after the Form of that of Loretto; and the Bowels in the Cathedral Church of St. Stephen. About 10 a Clock this evening the remainder of the Body will be carried to the Church of the Capucin Fryers, and there buried in a Vault built by the Emperor Mathias, where all his Poſterity lie interred.

Francfort, May 17. Letters from Prince Eugene's Camp near Verona of the 8th, and from Trent of the 10th Inſtant, ſay, a Detachment of his Forces had defeated a Body of 500 of the Enemy near Iſola della Scala, and taken 200 Priſoners. The Imperial Army which is to be commanded by Prince Lewis continues to draw together near Lauterbourg.

Hague, May 22. N. S. Letters from Coblentz of the 17th Inſtant give an Account, That his Grace the Duke of Marlborough was arrived there, and intended to go on the 19th to Creutznach to meet Prince Lewis; and it is believed, his Grace may be at Triers this day or to morrow. According to our Advices from the Maeſe, Monſieur d'Auverquerque was ſtill encamped near Maeſtricht with the Army under his Command, and was fortifying the Avenues to his Camp, intending, in all probability, to remain there till he ſees what the Enemy intend to do, who have at preſent the Superiority in Number, having ſent no new Detachments of late towards the Moſelle. Their Forces are now poſted in ſmall Bodies along their Lines, and ſo diſpoſed, that they may draw together whenever they ſhall ſee occaſion. The Elector of Bavaria is not yet come to their Army, the Jealouſies and Miſunderſtanding continuing between him and the Marſhal de Villeroy. A Party of the Gariſon of Breda fell lately into an Ambuſcade of Bavarian Dragoons and Huſſars, and having ſurrendred themſelves Priſoners, upon Promiſe of having Quarter given them, were afterwards all murdered in cold Blood by the Enemy, except 8. Monſieur d'Auverquerque has ſent a Complaint thereof to the Marſhal de Villeroy, acquainting him at the ſame time, That if Satiſfaction be not given, he will cauſe all the Priſoners that ſhall fall into our Hands to be put to the Sword. The Dutch Squadron from the Texel, commanded by Admiral Allemonde, having been joined by the Squadrons from the Maeſe and from Zealand, ſailed from the Goree two days ago. The Earl of Portland arrived here this morning from England. His Grace the Duke of Norfolk arrived here laſt night from his Travels, and purpoſes to go over into England in 3 or 4 weeks.

Falmouth, May 12. The Prince Packet Boat arrived here yeſterday, being come in 15 days from Lisbon: The Commander reports, That the Portugueſe have retaken the Town of Salvaterra, which had been taken by the Enemy the laſt Campaign; and that Sir John Leake was ſtill at Lisbon with the Squadron under his Command, except ſome of Her Majeſty's Ships that were out a cruiſing, and others that were gone out to convoy two Fleets of Merchant-men.

Plimouth, May 11. The 9th Inſtant Her Majeſty's Ship the Triton brought in here as Prize a French Privateer of 26 Guns.

Portſmouth, May 15. Sir Clowdeſly Shovell, Rear-Admiral of England, and Commander in Chief of Her Majeſty's Fleet, and Sir John Jennings, Rear-Admiral of the Blue, arrived here the 13th Inſtant in the evening, and immediately went off to Spithead; the Cannon on our Platform being diſcharged. Sir Clowdeſly Shovell hoiſted his Flag on board the Britannia, and was ſaluted by a Diſcharge of the Cannon of all the Men of War; and Sir John Jennings hoiſted his Flag on board the Royal Anne.

Kenſington, May 13. On the 11th Inſtant the Count de Gallas, Envoy Extraordinary from the Emperor, received an Expreſs from the Imperial Court, which proceeded afterwards towards Portugal, with the melancholy News of the Death of the late Emperor Leopold, and the Acceſſion to the Imperial Throne, of the preſent Emperor Joſeph, the Firſt of that Name; which he notified yeſterday, according to the Orders he had received in that Behalf, to Her Majeſty in a private Audience, to which he was conducted by Sir Charles Cottrell, Maſter of the Ceremonies: He aſſured Her Majeſty at the ſame time, in the Name of the New Emperor, That he would not only obſerve religiouſly all the Treaties concluded with his late Predeceſſor of Auguſt Memory, but that he would omit nothing that may render thoſe Alliances more firm and ſtrict, till that End is gained which was therein propoſed for the Good and Safety of the Common Cauſe; All which was confirmed by a Letter of Notification from his Imperial Majeſty, which the Envoy delivered at the ſame time to Her Majeſty. He afterwards had Audience of his Royal Highneſs, being likewiſe Introduced by Sir Charles Cottrell, Maſter of the Ceremonies.

Members

Figure 53
The London Gazette. 1705.
Source: Wikimedia.

Magazines

Periodicals catering to a broad readership began being published in the eighteenth century. Among the early magazines were the *Tatler*, the *Rambler*, and the *Spectator*, all published in London in the earlier eighteenth century. The *Gentleman's Magazine*, published from 1731 to 1911, introduced the word *magazine*. Benjamin Franklin published the first issue of his *General Magazine* in Philadelphia in 1741.

In the nineteenth century, cheaper magazines were printed, using all the newest technologies to draw audiences in. The *Illustrated London News*, for example, always carried color illustrations of notable events; the *Penny Magazine* "for the diffusion of useful knowledge" brought cheap information to a very wide audience (Figure 54). The later nineteenth century saw an explosion in the production of magazines, many of them aimed at new readerships of popular literature—women, in particular. *Godey's Lady's Book*, for example, was the highest-circulation magazine in the United States before the American Civil War. Published from 1830 to 1878, it contained articles on crafts, dance, health, and hygiene; biographies of famous people; and sheet music for the pianoforte. Fashion magazines, lifestyle magazines, and magazines catering to specialist interests all emerged in this period, continuing in popularity throughout the twentieth century. Sold at newsstands and in stationers or delivered by mail, the magazine in its manifold formats had enormous cultural reach. Now, with the emergence of online magazines and digital versions of analog magazines, the printed magazine is in decline.

QUESTIONS

1. What is the typical layout of a magazine? Flick through the digital version here: https://archive.org/stream/ThePennyMagazineOf TheSocietyForTheDiffusionOfUsefulKnowledge1844#page/n11 /mode/2up.

2. What was *Poor Richard's Almanack*, and who published it? What is its modern equivalent?

3. What inventions facilitated the production of cheap newspapers and books in the nineteenth century?

4. What is the role of advertising in the production of magazines?

5. Research sales figures on magazines. What predictions about the longevity of this form of text technology can you make?

FURTHER READING

Angeletti, Norberto, and Alberto Oliva. *Magazines That Make History: Their Origins, Development, and Influence.* Gainesville: University of Florida Press, 2004.

Brooker, Peter, and Andrew Thacker, eds. *The Oxford Critical and Cultural History of Modernist Magazines.* Vol. 1: *Britain and Ireland, 1880–1955.* Oxford: Oxford University Press, 2009.

Haveman, Heather A. *Magazines and the Making of America: Modernization, Community, and Print Culture, 1741–1860.* Princeton, NJ: Princeton University Press, 2015.

Summer, David E. *The Magazine Century: American Magazines since 1900.* Amsterdam: Peter Lang, 2010.

Wood, James P. *Magazines in the United States.* New York: Ronald Press, 1971.

Hathi Trust, Digital Penny Magazine: https://babel.hathitrust.org/cgi/ pt?id=inu.30000093220105;view=1 up;seq=1

A History of the Gazette: http://bit .ly/13miKsW.

Figure 55

The Spectator. 1711.

Source: Elaine Treharne.

The *Spectator*

The *Spectator* was not the first newspaper, but it was among the first relatively inexpensive texts that people read six days a week in order *not* to get the news. What the *Spectator* (Figure 55) offered its readers was not information but the potential to cultivate a certain disposition and advertise a kind of taste. It was a wildly successful publication, and its prose was taught for over a century in English schools as the apogee of urbane and polished written English.

Joseph Addison, cofounder of the *Spectator* in 1711, reckoned in an early number that although circulation was at 3,000 copies per issue, about twenty people read each copy. While this is probably an exaggeration, it speaks to the situation in which the magazine was read: in London's new and enormously popular coffeehouses. Men and women (though mostly men) gathered in these establishments, drank the novel and invigorating brew, and debated the news of the day (which often did not rise to the level of what might today be called "news" by an establishment publication like the *New York Times*) with one another. Contrary to our experience of a coffeehouse today, in which we might sit with a laptop for three hours and speak to no one while nursing a latte, the coffeehouse in Addison's day was an entirely social and discursive place where patrons expected to converse with a loosely affiliated band of near-strangers and mild acquaintances. Different coffeehouses had different focuses (e.g., poetry, foreign affairs, science), and patrons might move from house to house picking up the variety of news that suited them. The *Spectator* mimicked this by putting different kinds of news and gossip under the appropriate coffeehouse heading.

FURTHER READING

Addison, Joseph. "'Introducing Mr. Spectator." March 1, 1711. Spectator Project @ Rutgers. http://bit .ly/148JFHK.

Bond, Donald F. "The Spectator." *Newberry Library Bulletin* 8 (1952): 239–41.

QUESTIONS

1. Look at Figure 55. How does the layout reflect its functionality?

2. Read online the first number of the *Spectator*, titled "Introducing Mr. Spectator." What can you infer about the conditions that made the character of Mr. Spectator possible? Why would Addison's contemporaries care about such a fictional character?

3. The *Spectator* was printed on paper that is over 13 inches long and about 9 inches wide. Why does this size matter?

4. What evidence does a text like the *Spectator* give us for how its writers conceived of society?

FURTHER READING

DeMaria, Robert. *Johnson's Dictionary and the Language of Learning.* Chapel Hill: University of North Carolina Press, 1986.

Lynch, Jack. *Samuel Johnson's Dictionary.* New York: Atlantic Books, 2004.

Lynch, Jack, and Anne McDermott, eds. *Anniversary Essays on Johnson's Dictionary.* Cambridge: Cambridge University Press, 2005.

Reddick, Allen. *The Making of Johnson's Dictionary.* Cambridge: Cambridge University Press, 1990.

Johnson's *Dictionary* Online: http://johnsonsdictionaryonline.com/.

Samuel Johnson's *A Dictionary of the English Language*

Johnson completed his dictionary in 1755 after nine years of work. (It is digitized and described in full at http://johnsonsdictionaryonline.com/page-view/). It was not the first dictionary of its kind in English, but it became the standard work until the publication of the *Oxford English Dictionary* in 1928. Johnson's massive reference work numbered 2,338 pages in two volumes. It was printed in red and black ink and costly to produce, even in an edition of 2,000 (it is a classic example of a book produced by a conger, or syndicate, of booksellers). The format was a very large folio, over 18 inches high. The binding was in calf with gilt, red, and green leather labels and raised bands, and it was expensive. Johnson's greatest innovation was to make his dictionary citational rather than definitional: he offered literary examples of every word he could, which added up to about 114,000 citations for just over 40,000 words.

QUESTIONS

1. Look online for a first edition of Johnson's *Dictionary* available for sale. Why do you think it is so expensive?

2. Who would have bought this text originally?

3. Why would anyone have bought this text? What would its contemporary equivalent be?

4. What other texts you've already looked at in this book remind you of Johnson's *Dictionary*, and why?

Denis Diderot and Jean le Rond d'Alembert's *Encyclopédie*

Just as lexicographic efforts like Samuel Johnson's sought to make all the words in a language accessible to readers in the eighteenth century, so too did other scholars seek to classify and make available the entirety of human knowledge. One of the most famous encyclopedias was that of Denis Diderot and Jean le Rond d'Alembert. (The *Encyclopédie* is fully translated at https://quod.lib.umich.edu/d/did/ and available with commentary at https://encyclopedie.uchicago.edu/.) Other encyclopedists, from Peter Ramus to Ephraim Chambers and Britannica to Diderot himself, tried to organize all of human knowledge as a tree. This Tree of Knowledge had all studies arranged in "containing" sets. So Diderot's *Encyclopédie* classified "calculus" as "Reason < Philosophy < Science of Nature < Mathematics < Pure < Arithmetic < Algebraic < Infinitesimal."

Like Johnson's *Dictionary* (see the previous entry), the *Encyclopédie* was very much a statement text, undertaken and purchased for what it said about the producers and the disseminators. Like the Voynich manuscript too, the *Encyclopédie* was valuable at least in part because of the cachet that ownership conferred on owners.

The *Encyclopédie* dwarfed even Johnson's *Dictionary* in size. Published in twenty-eight volumes between 1751 and 1772 with over 70,000 entries, publication rights were bought by the French writer and publisher Charles-Joseph Pancoucke, who continued to expand the work into the nineteenth century, where it ended up with over 160 volumes. The *Encyclopédie* aimed to transform the intellectual culture of its time. Its astronomical cost and dizzying logistical challenges ended the careers of many of the people who tried to produce it.

FURTHER READING

Darnton, Robert. *The Business of Enlightenment: The Publishing History of the "Encyclopédie," 1775–1800.* Cambridge, MA: Harvard University Press, 1979.

Yeo, Richard. *Encyclopaedic Visions: Scientific Dictionaries and Enlightenment Culture.* Cambridge: Cambridge University Press, 2001.

The *Encyclopedia* of Diderot and d'Alembert: https://quod.lib.umich.edu/d/did/.

QUESTIONS

1. How concerned were the editors of the *Encyclopédie* with dissemination?
2. What political consequences might be attributed to the *Encyclopédie*?
3. Can you identify a more effective way of formulating and delivering this text?
4. Look at the Tree of Knowledge that the *encyclopédistes* tried to adhere to. How does the *Encyclopédie* try to authenticate itself? What is the relationship between form and content?

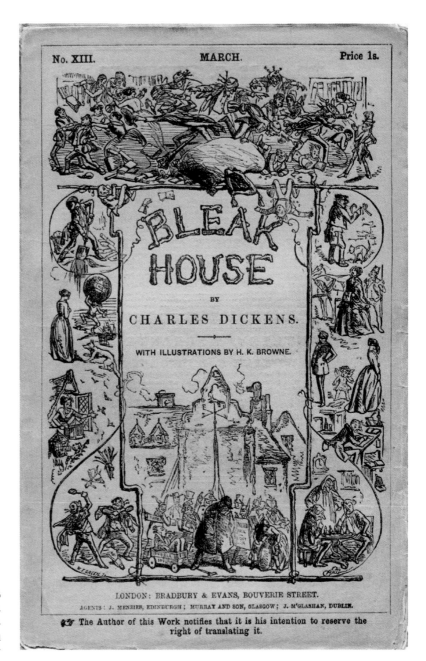

Figure 56
Charles Dickens's *Bleak House.*
1852–53.

Source: Courtesy Department of Special
Collections, Stanford Libraries.

Charles Dickens's Writing*

Charles Dickens is one of the most famous novelists in English, yet he didn't write books as such. Like the majority of other novelists in the nineteenth century, Dickens published his narratives in serial form, in sequential parts according to a schedule. Many such novels originally appeared in periodicals or magazines. *Bleak House* was published in monthly installments over two years (1851–52). Each installment came with a blue wrapper (like the one seen in Figure 56), printed on the inside with publishers' advertisements, and contained thirty-two pages (two octavo sheets) of text, including illustrations by Dickens's collaborator, Hablot Browne, also known as Phiz.

Periodicals and serial installments were more affordable than complete books and therefore reached a wider and more economically diverse readership. Serial publication also affected the narrative, as authors shaped installments to maintain readers' interest over the long term, sometimes making changes on the fly based on how the work was being received. After the issues were finished, publishers typically offered bound-volume versions of the complete text, stripped of its paratextual elements like this wrapper (now very rare). Many authors also revised their texts before publication in traditional book format.

FURTHER READING

Altick, Richard D. "Nineteenth-Century English Periodicals." *Newberry Library Bulletin* 9 (1952): 255–64.

Brattin, Joel. "Project Boz: Dickens and Serial Fiction." https://digitalcommons.wpi.edu/dickens-novels/.

Mott, Frank Luther. *American Journalism: A History: 1690–1960.* New York: Macmillan, 1962.

QUESTIONS

1. In the nineteenth century, in what form were the majority of novels originally published?
2. How might the serial or sequential publication of novels have affected the way they were written?
3. What textual difference does it make to republish a serial text as a single entity?

* This entry was written by Paul Fyfe, North Carolina State University.

FURTHER READING

Hoare, Peter, ed. *The Cambridge History of Libraries in Britain and Ireland.* 3 vols. Cambridge: Cambridge University Press, 2006.

Lerner, Fred. *The Story of Libraries: From the Invention of Writing to the Computer Age,* 2nd ed. London: Bloomsbury, 2009.

Manguel, Alberto. *A History of Reading.* New York: Penguin 1997.

——. *The Library at Night.* New Haven, CT: Yale University Press, 2008.

Martin, Lowell A. *Enrichment: A History of the Public Library in the United States in the Twentieth Century.* London: Scarecrow Press, 1998.

Watson, Paula D. "Founding Mothers: The Contribution of Woman's Organizations to Public Library Development in the United States." *Library Quarterly* 64 (1994): 238–45.

Wiegand, Wayne. *Main Street Public Library: Community Places and Reading Spaces in the Rural Heartland, 1876–1956.* Iowa City: University of Iowa Press, 2011.

Readers and Reading

Although throughout the course of this book, we insist on the multiple media by which text can be consumed, the majority of text technologies are designed to be read, either in silence or aloud. The ability to read, literacy, is highly prized to the extent that illiteracy is heavily stigmatized and can even seem shocking today.

The history of reading and libraries, providing access to texts, is rich and long. The earliest libraries, like that at Alexandria (third century BCE), sought to be national repositories of all the world's knowledge. Libraries subsequently have become the personal, local, or national organizers of human textual effort, as well as a place of respite and community; they are the sites of individuals' efforts to collect and preserve, and buildings that contain remarkable specialist and rare textual or artistic materials. In nineteenth-century America, the town's library, usually funded by Andrew Carnegie, was found on Main Street, among other main civic buildings. Alongside the history of libraries is the history of a reading public, whose preferences and mores are reflected in the books and music purchased and borrowed. Increasingly, the role of libraries and bookshops has expanded, with more flexible spaces, often devoted less to texts and more to information provision and communal learning environments.

QUESTIONS

1. What is the role of the library in contemporary life?
2. What is the role of the bookshop—if, indeed, it has a role in today's society?
3. Do you read? What does this question usually mean when it is asked? Why? What kinds of answers do you give?
4. If you go into a library or bookshop, what do you need to know to access texts? How are texts arranged? What texts do bookshops sell?
5. What is the role of Amazon.com or AbeBooks in the dissemination of text technologies? How have (and will) these large companies affect our reading habits?

Figure 57
Marsh's Library. 1707.

Source: Marsh's Library, by Tim Tregenza,
is licensed under CC BY-SA 3.0. https://
commons.wikimedia.org/w/index.php?se
arch=marsh+library&title=Special%3ASe
arch&go=Go#/media/File:Marsh%C2%B4s
library-_panoramio.jpg.

The Marsh Library

The first public library in Dublin, Marsh Library, was founded in 1708 by Archbishop Marsh next to Saint Patrick's Cathedral. The library's approach to protecting its books was to require readers to sit in cages while they consulted texts (Figure 57). The cages obviously didn't have the desired effect, however, since in 1777, the library issued an edict that all books, except especially small or valuable books, had to be consulted at a large central table in the library.

FURTHER READING
Marsh Library website: http://www
.marshlibrary.ie/.

QUESTIONS

1. What approach to the role of reading in a society do the cages show? Do they show knowledge as cheap or expensive? Safe or dangerous?

2. What can you deduce from the reversal of policy on cages in 1777? What equivalent technologies do we have today?

FURTHER READING
Bodleian Libraries website: http://www
.bodleian.ox.ac.uk/.

Duke Humfrey's Library

Duke Humfrey's Library in Oxford was founded by Duke Humfrey of Gloucester in the 1430s and was last expanded in 1637. It is now the oldest part of Oxford University's Bodleian Library. Duke Humfrey's was a chained library, meaning that the spines and covers of the books were literally chained to a rod attached to the shelves to prevent the books from being removed and ensure their durability as a scholarly resource. The books were also stored with their spines facing inward and with numbers on the exposed pages of the books. Concealing the spines meant that scholars couldn't tell which books were which unless they bought a catalog that identified which numbers corresponded to which books.

QUESTIONS

1. What sort of learning environment was Duke Humfrey's Library in the seventeenth century?
2. What kind of university system does a library with these technologies fit into best? Why do we not use these technologies now?
3. What did scholars and students go to the library for when it was first built (and through to the early twentieth century)?

FURTHER READING
Leapman, Michael. *The Book of the British
Library.* London: British Library, 2012.
British Library website: http://www.bl.uk/.

The British Library

Britain's national library occupies a large site in central-north London (Figure 58). It houses many of Britain's greatest literary treasures, including many ancient Buddhist scrolls, the world's oldest dated printed book (the Diamond Sutra), the Magna Carta, the Lindisfarne Gospels, the Codex Vaticana and part of the Codex Sinaiticus, and letters and manuscripts from prominent national figures. It has some of the original lyrics of Beatles' songs, music, and scrolls and many of the greatest literary works. As a copyright library, it receives a free copy of everything published in the United Kingdom, and it has vast storage in Boston Spa in Yorkshire. It currently houses over 150 million items. At the center of the library is the King's Library, given by George II in 1752 and supplemented by his son George III's enormous posthumous donation in 1823. There are many separate reading rooms with space for twelve

Figure 58
The British Library, main atrium.
Twentieth century.

Source: Elaine Treharne.

hundred readers. The library has a café and a restaurant in the central lobby. The entire library is built around the four-floor glass tower of the King's Library.

In recent years, the British Library has been in the vanguard of digital projects, including digital preservation, curation, and display. As with many other libraries around the world, the digital realm is demanding new methods in research and textual practice.

Spend some time browsing the website, particularly with regard to the British Library's digitized materials and its digitization strategy (http://www.bl.uk/aboutus/stratpolprog/digi/digitisation/).

QUESTIONS

1. What kind of text technology is the British Library itself?
2. To what kind of society does the British Library cater?
3. What approach to knowledge does the British Library's physical structure imply?
4. What relationship between nationhood and knowledge does the library imply?
5. What kinds of activities go on in a library: reading, writing, disputation?

Sound and Image

The Zoetrope

FURTHER READING

Burns, Paul. "The History of the Discovery of Cinematography." N.d. http://www.precinemahistory.net/.

The zoetrope (Figure 59), an important antecedent of cinema, was invented by William Horner in 1834. It is a drum printed with a sequence of images between slits through which a viewer peers while turning the drum. The faster the drum is turned, the more smoothly the sequence of images runs until it begins to resemble animation. Popular images included a running horse and a frog bouncing a ball.

QUESTIONS

1. Does the zoetrope convey information? Does it convey meaning as a technological form?
2. What are the prerequisites for a technology like the zoetrope?
3. If a new technology is developed largely as a toy, what does that say about its originating society?

Figure 59
Zoetrope, Leeds Industrial
Museum. Nineteenth century.

Figure 60
Still from *Arrival of a Train at
La Ciotat*. 1895.

Source: http://www.moma.org
/collection, Louis Lumière

Film

Film first came to the fore between 1892 and 1894, when it was silent, with a fairly low frame rate. The technology continued to innovate, adding sound, higher frame rates, color in increasing degrees of richness, and, more recently, the illusion of a third dimension. In that it is watched in a theater, cinema is the descendant of drama and opera. It is a technology designed for public consumption. Film is meant to be affordable mass entertainment, with all the implications of those words. Figure 60 shows a still from Auguste and Louis Lumière's *Arrival of a Train at La Ciotat*, filmed in 1895. (The film is available at https://www.youtube.com/watch?v=1dgLEDdFddk.)

The cinema has been one of the most significant forms of text technologies since its origins in the nineteenth century. Today, despite the ability of all smartphone users to create their own film experiences and despite the mass appeal of television, YouTube, and other means of sound-image transmission, cinema remains a very particular community experience, with a multibillion-dollar industry behind it.

QUESTIONS

1. What sorts of texts are well suited, and not well suited, to the technology offered by film?

2. Are there media earlier in history that permitted anything like the possibilities that film represents? Why or why not?

3. What does the advent of film (and other forms of mass entertainment) say about the status of leisure time?

4. What potential for the play of authority of any kind does film afford?

5. Think about the debate that rages every time a revered book is adapted for film. What does this reveal about our attitudes to textual adaptation and about the forms of textual authority to which we become attached?

FURTHER READING

Adorno, Theodor, and Max Horkheimer. *The Dialectic of Enlightenment*. Stanford, CA: Stanford University Press, 2002.

Burch, Noël. *Life to Those Shadows*. London: British Film Institute, 1990.

Fortmueller, Kate. "Arrival of a Train." *Critical Commons*. N.d. http://www.criticalcommons.org/Members/kfortmueller/clips/arrival-of-a-train-aka-l2019arrivee-d2019un-train.

Hazanavicius, Michel. *The Artist*. Dir. Michel Hazanavicius, Studio 37, 2012.

Kaufman, Charlie. *Adaptation*. Dir. Spike Jonze, Columbia, 2002.

Loiperdinger, Martin. "Lumière's Arrival of the Train: Cinema's Founding Myth." *Moving Image* 4 (2004): 89–118.

Rossell, Deac. *Living Pictures: The Origins of the Movies*. Albany: State University of New York Press, 1998.

Stam, Robert. *Film Theory: An Introduction*. Oxford, UK: Blackwell, 2000.

Williams, Linda, ed. *Viewing Positions: Ways of Seeing Films*. New Brunswick, NJ: Rutgers University Press, 1994.

FURTHER READING

Abramson, Albert. *The History of Television, 1942 to 2000.* Jefferson, NC: McFarland, 2003.

Fisher, David E., and Marshall J. Fisher. *Tube: The Invention of Television.* Washington, DC: Counterpoint, 1996.

Janowitz, M. "Sociological Theory and Social Control." *American Journal of Sociology* 81 (1975): 82–108.

Sorkin, Aaron. *West Wing.* NBC, 1999–2006.

Webb, Leicester. "The Social Control of Television." *Australian Journal of Public Administration* 19 (1960): 193–214.

Williams, Raymond. *Television: Technology and Cultural Form.* New York: Routledge, 2003.

Television

Invented in the 1920s but not widespread until the 1950s, television offers the possibilities of film transposed from a public space to a private space. Until the 1960s, viewers watched programs in black and white on small screens with a very limited choice of channels. Color was then introduced, and in the early 2000s, digital television and high-definition resolution dramatically changed viewers' experiences.

From the 1950s to the 2000s, television was probably the most significant form of information dissemination in the West. Consumers of TV watch more than consumers of film do, hour for hour, and they have more control over what they choose to watch. Producers of text for TV also have readier access to adaptive technologies than do producers of film and are more likely to be permitted by consumers to intersperse black and white with color, long takes with quick cuts, or silent with talkie. The whole issue of televisual viewing has become more complex in recent years, with multiple devices (laptops, tablets) being used to display programs originally intended for the television screen.

QUESTIONS

1. How do the various major changes in television's technologies—from small screens to large, wall-mounted televisions; terrestrial broadcasting to satellite; black and white to color; video to film—alter the ways in which viewers experience programs?

2. Consider sedimentation broadly (see Part 1). When, during an address, the president speaks directly to the camera in one long take, that is a use of sedimented text technology, dating in part to when broadcasters could afford only one camera. How do different programs you watch make different claims to authority? Consider, for example, news anchors, meteorologists, sportscasters, and location reporting.

3. What other text technologies have moved from public to private? What kinds of social forms are relegitimated by the advent of a private adaptation of a public technology?

Radio

Radio, or wireless telegraphy (arguably invented by Guglielmo Marconi in 1895) was originally a sequence of Morse code messages sent between correspondents, most often used to communicate with ships. After World War I, radios became popular in households and quickly became the most significant form of information provision. Important companies like the British Broadcasting Corporation and AT&T were founded in the 1920s with the sole rights to broadcast—a monopoly that lasted for decades. The 1920s to the 1950s is considered radio's Golden Age. Throughout this period and culminating in the 1960s, pirate radio was a significant phenomenon, with unregulated stations, such as Radio Caroline, broadcasting from out at sea.

Radio technology remained relatively unchanged from the time that Marconi invented it in 1895 to the recent advent of digital radio less than a decade ago. While the substrate of radio has changed with digital radio, the tools are fundamentally the same and the resulting text is almost indistinguishable. As a text technology, radio is less immersive than film or TV because it stimulates only one sense rather than two. However, all the same versatility for the manipulation of authority is still there.

Radio's greatest strength is its enormous power of transmission. Radio waves with wavelengths of up to 62 miles enable some governments to stay in constant radio contact with their submarine fleets. The great distance that radio waves can travel makes it the most powerful, modular, and accessible technology, bar none, for transmitting information around our planet. The low cost of a radio receiver makes radio an ideal technology for any society that wants to reach and include any disparate group, whether military or social.

FURTHER READING

Federal Communications Commission. "A Short History of Radio: With an Inside Focus on Mobile Radio." Winter 2003–04. https://transition .fcc.gov/omd/history/radio /documents/short_history.pdf.

Gerbner, George. "Mass Media and Human Communication Theory." In *Human Communication Theory*, edited by Frank E. X. Dance, 40–57. New York: Holt, Rinehart and Winston, 1967.

Johns, Adrian. *Piracy: The Intellectual Property Wars from Gutenberg to Gates*. Chicago: University of Chicago Press, 2009.

Lewis, Peter M., and Jerry Booth. *The Invisible Medium: Public, Commercial, and Community Radio*. Washington, DC: Howard University Press, 1990.

Siepmann, Charles Arthur. *Radio, Television and Society*. Oxford: Oxford University Press, 1950.

UNESCO. "Innovative Radio: Inspiring Social Change!" N.d. http://bit .ly/15SbLv3.

United States Early Radio History: http:// earlyradiohistory.us/.

QUESTIONS

1. What sorts of texts are poorly suited to radio and what sorts excel?
2. How do censorship and cryptography work on radio?
3. Film, TV, and radio all have a distinct ratio of power between producer and consumer. What is that ratio?
4. Radio is not strictly speaking a sedimented technology, even though there exist text technologies that can disseminate more information. Why not?
5. Imagine that you live at the dawn of public and commercial broadcasting. How would listening to the radio change your understanding of your society?

Digital Technologies

BBSs and the WELL

Early bulletin board systems (BBS) were designed to resemble corkboards on which users could pin messages for one another. (This is another example of sedimentation.) As communities evolved, different corkboards, or just boards, were spun off into separate forums in which people posted.

The Whole Earth 'Lectronic Link (WELL), founded in 1985, was the prototype for all the online communities that we now take for granted. It is the oldest online community in continuous existence.

Neither the WELL nor the BBS operates like our contemporary equivalents, though there are occasional instances of sedimentation. (The Facebook wall harks back to a BBS format.) But they permitted entirely novel connections between agents who had never communicated before and were brought together by their substrates. Although Marshall McLuhan spoke in another context when he said that "the medium is the message," in the case of these early electronic communications, the simple fact of the connection between the agents was so unlikely and so apparently intimate that early users of these technologies would wonder (at length) at its implausibility. (Examine the website at http://www.well.com/.)

FURTHER READING

Brand, Stewart. *From Counterculture to Cyberculture: The Whole Earth Network, and the Rise of Digital Utopianism.* Chicago: University of Chicago Press, 2010.

Branscomb, Anne W. "Common Law for the Electronic Frontier." *Scientific American* 265 (1991): 154–58.

Rheingold, Howard. "Virtual Communities: Exchanging Ideas through Computer Bulletin Boards." *Whole Earth Review* (1987). https://journals.tdl.org/jvwr/index.php/jvwr/article/view/293/247.

Textfiles.com: http://textfiles.com.

QUESTIONS

1. How private are online forums like BBSs?

2. What is the relationship between dissemination and this text technology? Does dissemination control production?

3. How can, and do, sites like the WELL deal with the problematic issue of authority when the communicating agents may never meet in person or exchange any of the traditional tokens of trust? What guarantees were available in the 1980s?

HTML, CSS, and RSS

In terms of the World Wide Web, hypertext markup language (HTML), cascading style sheets (CSS), and really simple syndication (RSS) are three popular text technologies. HTML is a way of controlling the display of information to a consumer in a single text; CSS is a way of formatting the display of texts across a whole stable of documents; and RSS is a way of aggregating those pages of styled content and delivering them all to a consumer in one convenient package. (RSS feeds can and do override the source CSS, however.)

As text technologies, HTML and CSS are production tools, and RSS is a dissemination tool. HTML and CSS make sure that whichever tool a consumer is using to read a given text, the text will be consistent across platforms. HTML and CSS by definition foresee massive and possibly random dissemination, certainly in ways that a producer knows they cannot predict. RSS is a vast innovation in dissemination technology, however, because consumers choose what will be disseminated to them in advance.

FURTHER READING

Berners-Lee, Tim, and Daniel Connolly. "Hypertext Markup Language (HTML): A Representation of Textual Information and MetaInformation for Retrieval and Interchange." June 1993. w3.org.

Finneran, Richard J. *The Literary Text in the Digital Age.* Ann Arbor: University of Michigan Press, 1996.

Levinson, Paul. *Digital McLuhan: A Guide to the Information Millennium.* New York: Routledge, 2013.

Sutherland, Kathryn, ed. *Electronic Text: Investigations in Method and Theory.* Oxford: Oxford University Press, 1997.

Codecademy: http://bit.ly/15UGK9F.

QUESTIONS

1. What is the position of copyright in this arena of rapid and possibly uncontrolled dissemination?

2. How can HTML and CSS be used to establish authority or control a text's interpretation? What kinds of authority are almost totally lost on the web?

3. Consider the semantics of HTML and CSS tagging (e.g., <em>, <br>, <div>). How might we think about HTML and CSS, though they are technologies, as text in and of themselves? What kinds of texts are they?

4. What information do HTML and CSS carry about the new information age?

FURTHER READING

Bartlett, Jamie. *The Dark Net: Inside the Digital Underworld*. London: William Heinemann, 2014.

Cormode, Graham. "Key Differences between Web 1.0 and Web 2.0." *First Monday* 13, no. 6 (2008). http://firstmonday.org/article/view/2125/1972.

Hendler, J. "Web 3.0 Emerging." *Computer* 42 (2009): 111–13.

Keen, Andrew. *The Internet Is Not the Answer*. New York: Atlantic, 2015.

O'Reilly, Tim. "What Is Web 2.0? Design Patterns and Business Models for the Next Generation of Software." *Communications and Strategies* 1 (2007): 17–38.

Segaran, Toby, *Programming Collective Intelligence: Building Smart Web 2.0 Applications*. Cambridge, MA: O'Reilly Media, 2007.

Web 2.0

Web 1.0 was a relatively static landscape of TEXT: text, images, and links arranged by CSS and HTML. Although very elaborate websites could be constructed with these simple but highly modular tools, Web 1.0 was not an interactive format. A classic example of Web 1.0 is the as-yet-unreconstructed Space Jam website from 1996 (http://www.warnerbros.com/archive/spacejam/movie/jam.htm).

Web 2.0 incorporated front-end scripts to make a user's consumption of a text much more dynamic. Rather than having consumers reload a page to see fresh information, Javascript-powered sites display new information without refreshing. Rather than conceiving of web pages as static entities holding information among which a consumer moves, like turning the pages of a book, Web 2.0 makes frames into text portals, capable of bringing fresh information to a visually static site.

Web 1.0 was based on the premise that it was worth loading a series of single information-rich pages because consumers might have to dial up each time they wanted more text. Web 2.0 is predicated on the ubiquity of broadband. Running the web's software, the internet has arguably developed into the most significant text technology the world has known to date. Even as we type, information is disseminated at a rate that is unimaginably massive; information is updated faster than could possibly be absorbed. Critics claim that the dangers of the internet are greater than the benefits and that cybersecurity is a more pressing issue than it has ever been. But all of the features of this technology (speed, accessibility, capacity, apocalypticism, and anonymity versus authority) have been seen before in the life cycles of historical text technologies; the difference now is scale and reach.

QUESTIONS

1. What will Web 3.0 be like?

2. What is the substrate in this context? What are the tools? How do tools evolve in this context to take advantage of the potential of new substrates?

3. What texts do you still read in a Web 1.0 style? What sorts of texts are better suited to Web 2.0?

4. What sorts of texts do you imagine we will use Web 3.0 to access?

Figure 61
Tablet technologies.
Twenty-first century.

Touchscreen Tablets

The touchscreen tablet (Figure 61) is a text technology developed by converging capacitive technologies (developed in the 1960s) and the screen as initially developed for mobile telephones. It is a highly unusual technology in that the tool is our fingers and the substrate is a sophisticated sheet of touch-responsive glass coated in a transparent metal compound. Tablets are rich in sedimented technologies; witness, for example, the very existence of a keyboard function that you can pull up on a tablet to type. Nonsedimented uses of a tablet are the manipulative hand gesture that we use to zoom, pan, or scroll a text, and e-book designers are exploiting all of these affordances of the technology to develop dynamic and interactive publications in which readers can participate. Apps (applications) have enlivened the uses not only of the smartphone but also of the tablet; indeed, the two technologies are so similar that it is difficult to distinguish their characteristics and functionality.

Some technology developers believe that the tablet is the future of all text technologies, while other believe the form is already stagnating. Sixty million tablets were sold in 2011, for example, while in 2015 that figure was 47 million, according to the International Data Corporation. Tablets

FURTHER READING

Carrière, Jean-Claude, and Umberto Eco. *This Is Not the End of the Book: A Conversation Curated by Jean-Philippe de Tonnac*. London: Vintage, 2012.

Mims, Christopher. "Why Tablets Are the Future of Computing." *Wall Street Journal*, September 14, 2015. http://www.wsj.com/articles/why-tablets-are-the-future-of-computing-1442203331.

have also been widely cited as the reason that sales of physical books seemed to be declining; this debate has spawned a vast amount of angst-ridden and largely ill-informed commentary on the "death of the book."

QUESTIONS

1. What is the tablet's technological debt to the wax tablet? What social formations does it have in common with the wax tablet?

2. Do you think that we have yet constructed texts that take full advantage of the potential of the substrate of the tablet? Why or why not?

3. Find a text that you can consume with a tablet. How would you modify it to use the possibilities of the substrate better?

4. Is a tablet a good medium to create a text with? Is it better for creation or consumption? Why?

5. Many patents are registered for various kinds of touchscreen text technologies, but as with the wax tablet, there are almost no academic studies. Why is that? What is it about the substrate that defies analysis?

Proprietary Content Streams

One significant development in text technologies of the recent era is corporatization. Several companies have developed proprietary mediaspheres within which users can access and consume text and sometimes produce it too.[4] The goal of these mediaspheres is to monetize human interaction with TEXT to the maximum extent possible. Although many companies have created such mediaspheres, we discuss only the three created by the world's three highest-value companies, as shown in the table, at time of writing.

MEDIA SPHERES

APPLE	GOOGLE	MICROSOFT
Pages	Docs	Word
Numbers	Sheets	Excel
iCal	Google Calendar	Outlook Calendar
Apple Mail	Gmail	Outlook
Quicktime/iTunes	Google Play/ YouTube	Windows Media Player/ Silverlight
Safari	Chrome	Internet Explorer
Mac/iMac	Chromebook	"PC"
iPad	NA	Surface
Apple Music	Google Play	NA
iPod	NA	Zune
iPhone	Android	NA

Google's range of text technological interfaces indicates their prediction of the future of text technological development. Google's mediasphere is predicated on an internet connection, whereas Apple and Microsoft are predicated on hardware formats. Apple and Microsoft are placing their bets on a more sedimented imagination of this feature of text technologies. If a digital text's substrate is always, finally, an electromagnetic medium (a tape, a disc, another storage mechanism) and the tool is always a method of placing a series of charges on that medium that indicate binary states (+ or –), then the differences between these mediaspheres are twofold: most transparently, the nature of the interface through which those tools are manipulated, and perhaps more important, the location of the substrate itself.

A mediasphere like Google's is built around the idea that the physical location of the substrate is going to be increasingly irrelevant to the consumer of a text. Apple and Microsoft, however, have constructed their text ecologies around highly portable but imprintable substrates. For example, a Chromebook is a portable set of interfaces designed for internet connectivity with minimal local storage (minimal inherent substrate). Conventional laptops, however, have a readable/writable substrate incorporated into their physical structure.

These mediaspheres combine physical technological developments with legal mechanisms in order to lock consumers into them and make the frictional cost of changing proprietary content streams as high as possible. If a user wants to buy a text from a store within such a mediasphere—the only way that much text is available—it will often become necessary to stay within the mediasphere for every subsequent interaction with that text. If I buy a text from the iTunes store, I will have to do it from within iTunes itself, giving Apple my credit card details to do so. A music file would then be downloaded to my substrate in a proprietary format such as m4p. In order to consume this text on a different substrate from my computer, I would have to move it to another substrate manufactured by Apple: a phone, tablet, computer, or music player. And to prevent me from disseminating this text, the legal mechanism of digital rights management (DRM) would limit the transmission of that text to only devices that were registered (with the proprietor of the content stream) as mine.

What this labyrinthine episode illustrates is that within a mediasphere like this, governed by compatibility rules and DRM, the consumer of a text is serially disempowered from interacting with the text in any way other than that prescribed by its distributor. Thus, most proprietary distributors do not in fact sell their users a text but rather the right to download a text a given number of times. One might argue that this is a logical conclusion of text technological development under late capitalism: control over the creation and dissemination of a text is best exercised by preventing consumers from ever owning a text in the first place.

QUESTIONS

1. How does the phenomenon of the proprietary content stream reflect on second-order text technological concepts like censorship or cryptography?

2. What kind of authority is manufactured by a proprietary content stream? Who holds it?

3. Would you, if you created a text and wanted to transmit it in exchange for money, want to use a proprietary content stream to do so? Why, or why not?

RESEARCH QUESTIONS

New Text Technologies

Compile a list of ten or more new text technologies that have emerged in your lifetime.

1. Which of these new technologies have already come and gone?
2. Which of these new technologies have longevity, and why?
3. In what ways do the new technologies you have named contribute to the development of textual production?
4. What threats do these emerging technologies pose to more established technologies?
5. What are the roles of anonymity and centralized authority in these new technologies?
6. What are major defining characteristics of these new text technologies in terms of intentionality, materiality, and functionality plus cultural value?
7. What social, cultural, and technological roles do you envisage the large Silicon Valley corporations playing in the coming years?
8. Respond to this statement: "There is no such thing as invention; there are only new convergences of existing technologies."

Writing Systems

1. Define each of the following in one sentence:

   Pictogram
   Ideogram
   Syllabary
   Alphabet
   Logogram

2. Classify the following writing systems according to their type: pictogram, ideogram, syllabary, alphabet, or logogram:

Akkadian	*Mayan*
Cuneiform	*Japanese*
Latin	*Ethiopian*
Cherokee	*English*
Hieroglyphic	*Chinese*

Form

1. Define the following forms:

a. Book	f. Tablet
b. Scroll	g. Stele
c. Cassette	h. Codex
d. Broadside	i. Screen
e. Obelisk	j. Bracteate

2. What other forms of text technologies can you think of?

Substrates

1. What are the dates of the following objects, and from what are they made?

   a. Codex Argenteus
   b. Mawangdui silk texts
   c. Taj Mahal
   d. Dead Sea Scrolls
   e. American Declaration of Independence
   f. Gezer calendar
   g. Sarajevo Haggadah
   h. Undley bracteate
   i. Vindolanda tablets

    j. Nuntii Latini

    k. Kuthodaw Pagoda

    l. Kata Tjuta

    m. Rublev's icon of the Trinity

    n. SnapChat

    o. *The Pillow Book*

    p. *The Fantastic Flying Books of Mr. Morris Lessmore*

    q. St. Petersburg, Public Library Ms. Q. V. 1, 3

    r. Ikom Monoliths

    s. the Taylor Prism

    t. Tombstone of 'Abāssa Bint Juraij

2. Does the size of each of these instances of a text technology matter? If so, in what ways?

3. What other substrates exist? What is the most perfect congruence of tool and substrate you can think of, and what determines your choice?

4. What are the largest text technologies, and what are the smallest? How does size affect the functionality of a textual artifact?

Sample Tools and Materials

What part of the textual production process are the following used for? (Example: pumice—scraping vellum.) What do they have in common?

a. Stylus

b. Lapis lazuli

c. Quill

d. Brush

e. Iron gall

f. Verdigris

g. Needle

h. Pen

i. Typeface

j. Knife

k. Deckle

l. Cochineal

m. Bone folder

n. Mold

o. Lunellum

p. Vat

TRENDS, THEMES, AND ISSUES

A number of major themes, concepts, and trends have emerged from the discussion of the text technologies in Part 2. Think about the importance of the following large areas of investigation for any one or more technologies from the earliest period to the present. Is it possible to argue that all are present in all text technologies to a greater or lesser extent? Which are the most significant for analysis of the creation, operation, and affordances of these text technologies?

Remember: The main thesis is that all text technologies comprise intentionality, materiality, functionality +/– cultural value. Other important themes, concepts, and trends to consider in your work on text technologies might include:

Accessibility	*Mouvance*
Anonymity	*Networks of production*
Apocalypticism	*Originality*
Authenticity	*Permanence*
Authority	*Portability*
Authorship	*Replicability*
Capacity	*Scale or scalability*
Communications circuit	*Social constructivism*
Connectivity	*Speed*
Democratization	*Stability*
Ephemerality	*Storage*
Information retrieval tools	*Suspicion*
Interactivity	*Sustainability*
Language	*Technological determinism*
Literacy	*Transnationalism*
Longevity	

PART 3   CASE STUDIES

FOR PART 3, CASE STUDIES, we chose five highly distinctive texts in order to show in a focused way how text technologies can illuminate both everyday and highly unusual objects. These analyses are not meant to be exhaustive or final; instead, they demonstrate how thinking in the ways that we have suggested can open up new analytical possibilities and give you a vocabulary for understanding the total effect of a text as it draws on different conceptual frameworks. We hope you find that these provide useful suggestions for how you might go about analyzing text technological objects. We provide these case studies simply as thought pieces, and so have no directive questions here. Try to complete your own research foci and derive your own bibliographical data on these objects, as modeled in Part 2.

We chose the one-dollar bill, the Rosetta Disk, the Cyrus Cylinder, the Eagles' song "Hotel California," and William Morris's Kelmscott Chaucer. In each case, intentionality, materiality, functionality, and cultural value work together in unusually powerful ways, and each uses at least one second-order concept of text technologies to add to its effectiveness as a text. We chose ancient, modern, and futurological texts to suggest to you the great flexibility of the theoretical framework we have laid out.

THE ONE-DOLLAR BILL

The most effective texts are those that are most adapted to their function. The US dollar bill, perhaps one of the most successful texts in existence, remains the world's most held reserve currency, making it, by one measure at least, the world's most trusted—and therefore most effective—currency. But currency is largely a fiction; it is given its authority by the number of people who agree to believe in it and believe that a dollar is worth a certain quantity of goods or services. This is an arbitrary belief. The job of physical money is to make that belief seem rational by tying the value it claims to embody to a series of symbols of authority.

To work, money needs to be stable and trusted. It needs to be so trusted that most users of the text forget, or never even realize, that it is a text. The function of the dollar bill is its governing principle. All other factors work harmoniously to promote the trustworthiness of the text.

The material of the dollar bill is paper that is rich in cotton. Crane and Co., a papermaking company based in Massachusetts, specializes in high-end writing paper (including paper made purely of cotton), and it manufactures a cotton blend for the Treasury that is not commercially available. This makes the material much more difficult to imitate or forge. Cotton-based paper is stronger and more durable under adverse conditions. It also holds ink far better than paper made from wood pulp. What makes the dollar bill's material unusual even among high-quality papers is that while it is just under 75 percent cotton, the remainder is linen, a tough, light cloth derived from beaten flax. The presence of linen in a dollar bill is what gives the bill the longevity it needs for many years of daily transactions and the flexibility to be folded many times without fracturing.

The dollar bill measures 6.14 inches by 2.6 inches, with a thickness of 0.0004 inch. The bill is roughly the length of a hand and tall enough to rest between thumb and forefinger. It is made to be manipulated by hands. At the same time, its proportions are unusual and not found in any common writing materials, so that it is at once a convenient and a distinctive size. The note is printed by dry intaglio printing; the blank

Figure 62
Detail of the front of a one-dollar bill showing the fineness of engraving at the base of the letter "N" of the "ONE."

paper is pressed onto a steel plate whose engraved grooves hold ink, which is then transferred to the paper. Dry intaglio printing allows for extraordinary detail, fast drying, and minimal distortion. The close-up in Figure 62 shows the level of detail that the substrate can hold. This level of detail also helps to make the dollar bill difficult to imitate. After the note is printed back and front, the Treasury seal and serial numbers are overprinted; this accounts for the different (slightly more vibrant) shade of green on those features.

The content of the note itself is remarkable because a huge amount of information is packed onto this substrate. The note bears the legend "THE UNITED STATES OF AMERICA" and "ONE DOLLAR" on both sides. Each corner on the front reads "1." The front tells the user, "This Note Is Legal Tender for All Debts, Public and Private." The front also bears the portrait of George Washington, the reproductions of the signatures of the secretary of the treasury and the treasurer, serial numbers, the series date, plate-positioning information, and the location in which the bill

Figure 63
Front and reverse of a 2009
one-dollar bill.

was printed. Entwined around the "1"s are olive branches. The top of the bill reads "FEDERAL RESERVE NOTE," indicating the ultimate federal backing of the money. The seal of the secretary of the treasury has scales, a key, and thirteen stars, bearing above it the legend "WASHINGTON, D.C." The reverse displays the obverse and reverse of the Great Seal of the United States to the left and right of the word "ONE." Above "ONE" is the official motto of the United States—since 1956, "IN GOD WE TRUST." Complex geometric designs fill in much of the rest of the reverse.

The features we have briefly described evoke other structures of authority. In Figure 63, the letter "D" on the front corresponds to the subscription "CLEVELAND, OHIO." George Washington, the first president of the United States, is depicted in the center of the front of the bill. He gazes at the user from his official portrait looking assured, even challenging. The faithfulness and fine detail that etching gives its referent metonymically stand for the solid, reliable representation of the value given by the note in transactions. Not only does Washington's portrait recall the founding of America, but the continuity of the presence of his face on the bill itself (since the note took this form in 1869) signals the dollar's stability and reliability.[1] The seal of the treasurer combines the signs of justice (scales) and trust and security (a key) with a chevron—a military symbol—bearing thirteen stars representing the thirteen original colonies. Beneath the shield is "1789," the date that the Treasury was founded. The olive branches woven around the numerals "1" symbolize peace and plenty. The cartouches holding each numeral are a classical artistic framing device designed to dignify the object at their center by associating them with neoclassical art history and historical continuity more generally.

The signatures, themselves a performance of presence in absence, call back to the origin of paper currency as a signed promissory note, "PAYABLE ON DEMAND." Though the dollar bill doesn't say this, the representation of the handwritten inscriptions of the treasurer and secretary stands for the personal backing that these figures give to the currency. After all, trust, like mistrust, is contagious. It helps to put Washington squarely between the two heads of the Treasury and implies that all three stand behind the value of the text the user is holding.

The Great Seal on the reverse of the note is incongruous and unusual. The thirteen-stepped pyramid with its floating eye (called the Eye of Providence) was a symbol of the Masons and earlier of the Illuminati. We must consider the possibility that such an obscure symbol is included on the note precisely because the majority of users will not understand it. Most users of a text this deeply enmeshed in the fabric of a whole nation expect not to understand, may even be quite reassured not to understand, all of its features. Indeed, what better way to engender trust in an opaque, obscure financial system than to be open (at least symbolically) about that opacity? The Latin legend above the eye reads "ANNUIT CŒPTIS," meaning, "He [God] favors our undertaking." Beneath are the roman numerals for 1776, the date of the Declaration of Independence. Beneath the pyramid a banner bears the legend "NOVUS ORDO SECLORUM" (new order of the ages). The obverse shows an eagle, again representative of the nation, beneath a rosette of thirteen stars, holding in one claw thirteen olive leaves and in the other thirteen arrows, standing for unity in peace and in war, respectively.

Above the word "ONE" that links together apparently mystical and animalistic symbols is the motto "IN GOD WE TRUST." This is the only explicit reference to a religion on the note and performs a markedly dual function. The way that the letters are printed makes the line appear detached from its true referent, "THE UNITED STATES OF AMERICA." The result is that the motto appears to be of the money itself. The positioning of the word "GOD" between the two symbols of the United States and over the word "ONE" makes it appear to refer to either the country (nation as deity) or the idea of a unit of money (money as deity).

The textness of the dollar bill, then, is extraordinarily hybrid: it combines two languages, visual and textual content, allegory, portraiture, religion, signatures, several different methods of indexing, and explicit appeals to the history and prestige of the nation. In its sheer density of information and absolute recognizability, it is a model of design. The motto in the beak of the eagle on the reverse of the Great Seal, "E PLURIBUS UNUM" (out of many, one), refers not only to the political philosophy of democratic representation but to the idea of a modern and participatory economy: if you have many of these notes, the eagle remarks obliquely, we will all work together.

THE ROSETTA DISK

Paper burns, and it dissolves in water. Even gentle acids like ink will eat through it in time. Its great strengths as a substrate are its accessibility and ease of use. But to store information for a long time, paper needs to be specially made and specially stored. Acid-free paper, inscribed with acid-free inks, can last for many hundreds of years if kept dark, dry, and in a stable (preferably cool) range of temperatures.

Materiality is always an important consideration for a text's creators and consumers alike. The choice of substrate and tool will define and shape the text's life cycle. The Rosetta Disk, a project of the Long Now Foundation, is an exceptional text because of its unusual materiality. It is one of the world's most technologically distinct texts. The foundation was founded in 1996 and promotes "thinking on a 10,000-year scale." Accordingly, it wanted to make a text with a higher threshold of durability than anything paper could offer in order to produce the most long-term repository of information possible. The disk is the culmination of eight years of work and an outstanding technological achievement. It holds over 13,000 pages of text, documenting 1,500 distinct languages, and is just 2.8 inches in diameter. It does not use any encoding or image compression; it is completely analog.

If the most successful texts are those that are most closely matched with their purposes, then the Rosetta Disk is a very effective text indeed. The problem faced by the Long Now Foundation in making a durable and truly future-proof archive was the same as that faced by anyone trying to anticipate the future of information retrieval: How can we make this text accessible to future technologies, including those that we can't yet imagine? Most solutions to this problem devised by software engineers or data architects involve some kind of modularity or built-in flexibility to ensure cross-platform compatibility.

Instead, Long Now Foundation solved the problem quite brilliantly: they etched the information directly onto the disk in actual legible letters. The only technology needed to read the disk is an optical microscope: at 1,000 times magnification, all of the disk's information is readable. The disk is unaffected by water, wide temperature fluctuations, or electromagnetic radiation. It comes packaged in a spherical case 4 inches in diameter; the upper half is a solid hemisphere of optical glass, which provides some magnification, and the lower half is a solid piece of stainless steel. It has a hollow machined ribbon of stainless steel and a stylus for keepers of the disk to make notes on for posterity.

The front of the disk bears an inscription describing the back of the disk (Figure 64). The front is made of titanium, overlaid with a layer of oxidized titanium. Text is made to appear on the front of the disk by etching away the oxidation. The eight headline languages spiraling around the front of the disk include English, Spanish, Cyrillic, Cantonese, and Arabic. Each inscription reads "Languages of the World: This is an archive of over 1,500 human languages assembled in the year 02008 CE Magnify 1,000 times to find over 13,000 pages of language documentation." Within that spiral is a complete list of the languages archived on the disk divided by continent. In the center of the disk is an etching of a Peters projection of Earth. The projection shows what Europeans might consider the back of the planet (the image has Asia at its center); this is because that hemisphere contains the vast majority of the planet's population.

The documentation is stored on the back of the disk, electroformed in solid nickel applied to a silica core of the disk (Figure 65). Each page image is only 400 microns across, roughly the width of five human hairs. For the microengraving to be legible, a special font had to be developed using cross-hatching to fill in the middle of each letter. The project was in fact delayed while engraving on this scale—the smallest ever—was developed. Individual letters are nanometers tall, and the nickel plating is so small that it refracts light, giving a shimmering diffraction rainbow effect not dissimilar to a compact disk.

This text is unusual in that it is designed not to be transmitted except through time. It is a pocket-sized archive, designed to last for thousands of years, but not designed to facilitate convenient or constant access. In this sense, the Rosetta Disk is a text with almost opposite intentionality to the dollar bill, but some factors are held in common: both are designed to fit comfortably in a hand, both are meant to be unimpeachably trustworthy, and both are designed to be (within the parameters of their use) as durable as possible.

The Rosetta Disk takes its name from the Rosetta Stone and aims, like that stone, to enable language learning through parallel texts. The documentation contains translations in each language of a small number of texts, including the first chapter of the Book of Genesis and the UN Charter of Human Rights. The disk is etched with maps, texts, word lists, and grammars in an effort to make it representative, to some extent, of the

Figure 64
Front of the Rosetta Disk.

Source: Rosetta Project.

"great diversity of human experience as well as the incredible variety of symbolic systems we have constructed to understand and communicate that experience."[2]

Future-proofing on the scale undertaken by the foundation is unusual. One practical consequence of that future-proofing is to keep the intention and function of the text roughly identical for the foreseeable future. The closer intentionality and functionality are, the more reconstructable the creator's intention is for the user. In the case of this text, the creators aim to convey factual information about the physical, social, and demographic constitution of the world. Only under very particular circumstances, in other words, could this text function have something other than what its creators have intended. For example, if there were hundreds of such disks, the Rosetta Disk might conceivably be recontextualized as an event within a history of analog language archival. However, given the great cost of manufacturing each disk, currently between $10,000 and $25,000, this situation seems unlikely.

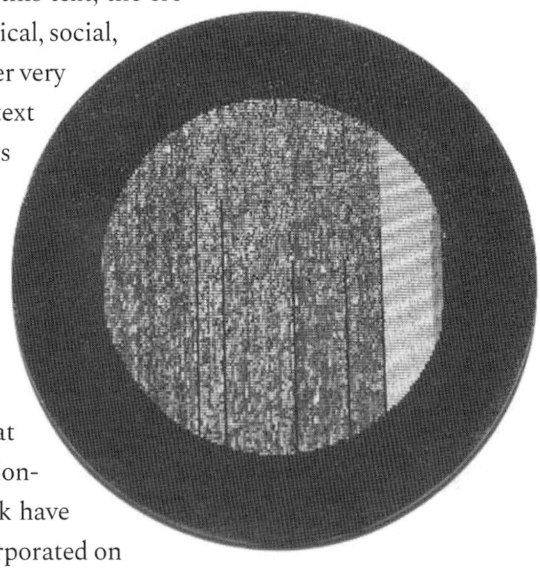

There are a few instances of data on the disk that might be vulnerable to the historical slippage of functionality away from intentionality. The makers of the disk have assumed that some of the texts and technologies incorporated on the disk are essential, native, intuitive forms when in fact they may not be. Maps, in particular, are complex spatial abstractions; the cartographic conventions governing the disk's heavily annotated maps are not necessarily enduring. Indeed, even the concept of a word list might become lost to linguists of the far future. So the disk is truly future-proof only insofar as our taxonomies of language and meaning are durable. A way to avoid this situation would be to invent a superordinate semantic code. But this is, of course, a fool's errand and far beyond the purview of innovative techno-archivists.

In other words, if a text is only as durable as our overall rules governing language organization, the creators of this text have succeeded in making as durable a text as could be imagined. Since texts are communicative

Figure 65
Reverse of the Rosetta Disk.
Source: Rosetta Project.

and communication is based on shared semantic codes, for a text even to face the specter of semantic obsolescence is for its creators to have utterly surpassed any ordinary limitations of materiality.

THE CYRUS CYLINDER

Cyrus's Persian Empire was, in 539 BCE, the largest ever seen on earth. It was the first multilingual, multifaith empire in the world when Cyrus captured Babylon, more or less without a struggle.

The Cyrus Cylinder (539) is a remarkable text that, despite its highly elaborate appearance and undeniable aura, was used as a foundation deposit, buried in the foundations of a building in order magically to inspire divine protection. The 2,600 years since its production have witnessed the growth of an immense gap between intentionality and functionality, between the reasons behind the creation of the cylinder and the uses to which it is put in the present day.

The cylinder has a core of gray stone, possibly granite, around which many layers of clay have been shaped to build up a large, oval-shaped cylinder.[3] An outer layer of soft wet clay was applied to the cylinder on which the inscription was made. The cylinder was then left to dry in the sun before being buried. It is 9 inches long, and 4¼ inches wide at its widest point. It was rediscovered in 1879 and broke during its excavation. The smaller fragment that was broken off at this time was lost and not rejoined to the main body of the cylinder until 1970, when it was loaned indefinitely to the British Museum by Yale University. Roughly a third of the cylinder remains missing, and most lines are incomplete or damaged.

The cylinder is primarily a religious text. Along with the core of his Persian Empire at Pasagardae, Cyrus was probably Zoroastrian. But the cylinder, created in Babylon following Cyrus's capture of the city, pays homage to a non-Zoroastrian deity, the Babylonian god Marduk: "Marduk, the great lord, bestowed on me as my destiny the great magnanimity of one who loves Babylon, and I every day sought him out in awe."[4] The cylinder was buried in the foundations of Esagila, a temple to Marduk. The job of this text is to procure Marduk's protection for a temple of Marduk in a city that largely worshipped the god.

The account of Marduk's conquests that the cylinder gives is in some ways conventional among accounts of conquering rulers: in many ways an unexceptional piece of propaganda extolling the virtue, clemency, and divinely anointed purpose of the conqueror. In particular, the cylinder recounts Cyrus's recent heroic acts, including (possibly) his freeing of the Jewish people whom Nebuchadnezzar and Belshazzar had enslaved. Whether Cyrus was Zoroastrian or not, it is a virtual certainty that he was not a Mardukian. But the cylinder praises Marduk because that makes the text better suited to its purpose. After all, what protection would Marduk give to a temple with foundation deposits that praised a different god altogether? How would Cyrus's new Babylonian subjects have looked on any other kind of foundation deposit?

Cyrus's freeing of the Jews, recounted far more fully in the Bible than on the cylinder, was probably a pragmatic decision: managing an enslaved population he inherited from his defeated opponent was likely to make him no friends and be costly and difficult. Freeing slaves would save administrative hassle and promote harmony within an empire that already contained those slaves' homelands. The pragmatism of Cyrus's act is further attested to by the discovery in 2009 of other cuneiform tablets in the British Museum recounting Cyrus's generosity in other parts of his empire. Cyrus is mentioned with great gratitude in the book of Ezra 1:1–8. The first four verses read:

Now in the first year of Cyrus king of Persia, that the word of the Lord by the mouth of Jeremiah might be fulfilled, the Lord stirred up the spirit of Cyrus king of Persia, that he made a proclamation throughout all his kingdom, and put it also in writing, saying, 2 Thus saith Cyrus king of Persia, The Lord God of heaven hath given me all the kingdoms of the earth; and he hath charged me to build him an house at Jerusalem, which is in Judah. 3 Who is there among you of all his people? His God be with him, and let him go up to Jerusalem, which is in Judah, and build the house of the Lord God of Israel (he is the God) which is in Jerusalem.

4 And whosoever remaineth in any place where he sojourneth, let the men of his place help him with silver, and with gold, and with goods, and with beasts, beside the freewill offering for the house of God that is in Jerusalem. (Ezra, 1:1–4)

Note that there is no Marduk here. The cylinder, however, is much more coy about this act of tremendous enfranchisement:

From [Shuanna] I sent back to their places to the city of Ashur and Susa, Akkad, the land of Eshnunna, the city of Zamban, the city of Meturnu, Der, as far as the border of the land of Guti—the sanctuaries across the river Tigris—whose shrines had earlier become dilapidated, the gods who lived therein, and made permanent sanctuaries for them. I collected together all of their people and returned them to their settlements, and the gods of the land of Sumer and Akkad which Nabonidus—to the fury of the lord of the gods—had brought into Shuanna, at the command of Marduk, the great lord, I returned them unharmed to their cells, in the sanctuaries that make them happy. (Cylinder, 30–34)

The Jews are never mentioned by name.[5] This is not necessarily to say that Cyrus did not free the Jews, but that even if the passage above does refer to that event, the terms in which we learn of Cyrus's repatriation of those displaced peoples are fairly simple and descriptive. There is no appeal, for example, to a larger philosophical justification for this decision.

In 1971, the 2,500th anniversary of the Cyrus Cylinder was celebrated with great fanfare and ceremony. The cylinder was adopted as a symbol of a united, powerful, prosperous, and enlightened Iran. When the cylinder was displayed for six months in Tehran, half a million people visited it. To this day, the cylinder appears on Iranian stamps and coins. In 1971, UN secretary general Sithu U Thant declared the cylinder to be an "ancient declaration of human rights," a claim that has been widely adopted by pro-Iranian bodies like the Iran Chamber Society. This nongovernmental organization exists to promote Iranian interests overseas and dedicates a web page to the cylinder.[6] The society claims that "there were three main premises in the decrees of the Cyrus Cylinder: the political formuliza- tion of racial, linguistic, and religious equality; slaves and all deported peoples were to be allowed to return to home; and all destroyed temples were to be restored."

The cylinder has become an especially potent symbol of Iranian reli- gious tolerance and Iranian-Jewish goodwill. The cylinder's visit to the Metropolitan Museum of Art in New York City was sponsored in part by the Iranian American Jewish Federation of New York. The cylinder was even referenced in a 2003 Nobel Peace Prize acceptance speech by Iranian laureate Shirin Ebadi:

> [Cyrus said] he would not reign over the people if they did not wish it. And [he] promised not to force any person to change his religion and faith and guaranteed freedom for all. The Charter of Cyrus the Great is one of the most important documents that should be studied in the history of human rights.[7]

There's no evidence, even on the cylinder, that Cyrus said this, though a spurious translation of the cylinder circulates online that includes lines like these. But such is the aura of the cylinder that a text like that above almost seems plausible.

This is the extent of the gap between intentionality and functionality in the case of this text: what was intended to serve as a piece of propa- ganda and provide divine protection for a temple has now become an emblem of forward-thinking enfranchisement and religious tolerance. That the nationality of this emblem has struggled to replicate that tol- erance and enfranchisement in the past forty years is not coincidental to our general desire to make the text a beacon of hope from the past. Whether the text's function as some currently regard it aligns at all with its original intention is a separate matter.

"HOTEL CALIFORNIA"

The texts we have discussed so far in this book have largely been visually apprehended. For many it is with our eyes that we receive most of our information about the world. But the rest of our sensorium should not be ignored. The tools and substrates of recorded music are nested, and complex to tease out: a plectrum is a tool and a string might be a substrate; a guitar connected to a microphone is a tool and a recording device a substrate; a turntable is a tool and a vinyl disc a substrate; and so on. But our analysis of musical texts can reveal their hybridity and sophistication: "Hotel California" blends together harmonic, lyrical, and visual texts.

The first track on the Eagles' fifth album, *Hotel California*, is also the title track, which indicates that it is intended to set the tone lyrically and musically for what is to follow. The lyrics of the song tell a tale, familiar to readers of the gothic genre, of a weary traveler who enters an apparently welcoming hostel only to find himself trapped forever in a bizarre and nightmarish place. The album cover very much bears out this sinister narrative.[8] The sunset behind the hotel silhouettes palm trees in front of it. The setting sun's rich gold is a photogenic tourist brochure cliché, but it also intimates a coming darkness. This darkness is picked up by the mass of foliage in front of the hotel, which obscures at least half of the structure in unilluminated growth. These bushes foreshadow the beast that the speaker sees stabbed in the hotel. The gloom of the bottom half of the picture is then ironized by the cheery neon sign at the base, which belongs again to the world of the tourist brochure (and the beach, an archetypal Californian location). The blue light of the sign picks up the blue lighting on the structure of the hotel itself, emphasizing its gothic architectural details such as cupolas and arches. As a text fitted to the lyrics of the song, the cover could not be more apt.

The musical structure of the song also exemplifies elements of the lyrical content. The song is built on an eight-measure chord progression for the introduction and verse. The chorus has a different eight-measure progression that eventually takes the harmony to the dominant key. The dominant key is natural point of return for the beginning of the verse, which begins again in the tonic, the home key. It is a founding principle of modern harmony (the harmony developed by Bach) that the dominant always leads back to the tonic: this is called a perfect cadence. A phrase that ends on the dominant is called an imperfect cadence, because it leaves the listener longing to return to the home key, the tonic.

The song proceeds in blocks of eight measures, like this:

Blocks	Section
2	Intro
2	Verse
1	[Chorus]
2	Verse
1	[Chorus]
2	Verse
5	Outro

The last words of the song, spoken by the Night Man to the Speaker at the close of the last section marked "Verse," are, "You can check out any time you like, / But you can never leave." So it is appropriate that this is not the end of the song. The guitar solo and duet (between Don Felder and Joe Walsh) that follow take a full forty measures—as much as the previous two verses and chorus combined. Moreover, the song doesn't ever actually end; the outro runs for four full blocks of eight measures and then begins to fade, taking a full eight measures to do so, performing structurally the inability to leave the hotel that the Night Man prophesizes. Furthermore, the last measure of the outro's five blocks of eight measures, and therefore the last measure of the song, is in the dominant key, so that the song ends, as it were, "imperfectly," leaving the harmonic structure unfinished. Harmonically, the song urges us to return again to its beginning, which is in the tonic.

Other elements of the music counterpoint pieces of lyrical content. Immediately following the speaker's climactic vision, "They stab it with their steely knives / but they just can't kill the beast," there is a marked ritardando (slowing down) punctuated by an aggressive drum fill. A moment after "beast" and before the beginning of the last stanza of the last

verse, the passage of time has seemed, however briefly, suspended or un-
certain. Whether the drum fill performs the stabbing knives or comments
ironically on the speaker's horrific sight, the slackening of the tempo
before it picks up again for the final stanza once again enacts the lyrics,
"Last thing I remember." The speaker's own experience of continuous
time has been interrupted, as has ours.

It is especially apposite that this text should have been released on
vinyl, a circular substrate that works by revolving around its center. Eagles
band member Don Henley said to *Rolling Stone*, "'Hotel California' was
our interpretation of the high life in Los Angeles,"[9] and the song's charges
of debauchery, meretriciousness, substance abuse, and self-righteousness
have been leveled at California, and specifically Los Angeles, many times
before and since. The woman who says to the song's speaker, "We are all
just prisoners here / Of our own device," speaks to the self-entrapment
of life in the Golden State and the circularity of the song's structures and
the text's substrate.

KELMSCOTT CHAUCER

For many of the texts mentioned in this book, aura or cultural value is an
important consideration, whether as a core component of intentionality
(the dollar bill) or functionality (the Cyrus Cylinder) or materiality (as in
textual objects made of parchment or gold). William Morris's Kelmscott
Press edition of *The Works of Geoffrey Chaucer* (1896) is an unusual modern
text in that it was created specifically to have a particular aura, in ways
and for reasons that will become clear. (Many pages from the work are
digitized at https://www.bl.uk/collection-items/the-kelmscott-chaucer.)

Morris was a nineteenth-century British designer and aesthete who
founded his own press "with the hope of producing some [books] which
would have a definite claim to beauty, while at the same time . . . not
dazzle the eye, or trouble the intellect of the reader by eccentricity of
form in the letters."[10] What this means is that Morris aimed at a perfect marriage of materiality and functionality. Whether his books man-
aged not to dazzle their readers with beauty is a matter for individual
judgment. Nevertheless, in the Kelmscott Chaucer Morris created an

extraordinary aura. Robert Milevski writes that Morris felt that the Industrial Revolution had "reduced the individual craftsmanship of ancient times to soulless formulas for the machine production of consumer objects without beauty or an inherent aesthetic."[11] In this, Morris anticipated Walter Benjamin, the great twentieth-century intellectual. Morris used heavily sedimented material technologies in the service of creating the greatest aura possible. He described himself as a socialist and wanted to work in the decorative arts in a way that redignified manual labor and its products.

Morris founded the Kelmscott Press in 1891 with the express purpose of building toward the Chaucer. He made an avid study of the fifteenth-century Venetian engraver Nicholas Jensen, a student of Gutenberg, and copied Jensen's roman font until he felt he could reproduce it by hand. Morris then designed his own font, based on Jensen's but influenced by fin-de-siècle design, which Morris named Troy. Morris next hand-cut a complete set of Troy in movable metal type and used it for the books he printed at his press.

Morris's material preparations for his Chaucer were particularly intense. He commissioned eighty-seven illustrations from Sir Edward Burne-Jones, his friend and fellow pre-Raphaelite artist.[12] Morris designed all other typographical elements of the book, including borders, initials, and title pages (Figure 66). He designed the watermark that the paper would have and insisted that the company that made the paper did so according to fifteenth-century papermaking methods. He concocted his own ink to replicate the deep black of Gutenberg's volumes but abandoned the idea of using his own inks for the whole run of Chaucer and had the ink specially formulated for him by a German firm. Morris used unusually large margins to offset his text, following the practice of manuscript scribes and early modern printers. After a trial run, he was dissatisfied with the font, Troy, and had it recut with the same forms but slightly smaller; this new form he named Chaucer. The whole run was hand-printed and took two years to print. Because the large margins required extraordinary pressure from the presses, Morris bought a larger and stronger press to handle the work.

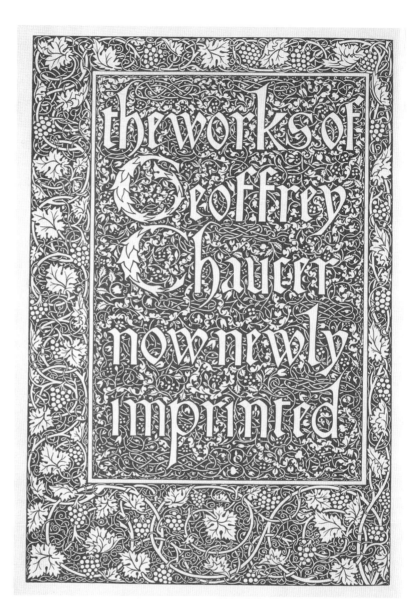

Morris printed 425 copies on his specially made paper. In an especially fetishistic decision, he even printed thirteen copies on vellum, or scraped calfskin. Vellum was a spectacularly expensive substrate in late nineteenth-century Britain, and the vellum copies were priced accordingly at £120, compared to £20 for the copy on handmade paper. Morris commissioned the Doves Bindery to design four different bindings in white pigskin with a silver clasp. One of these was chosen, and forty-eight copies were bound in it. The leather was elaborately hand-tooled beyond anything commonly practiced by the medieval binders Morris admired.

The Kelmscott Chaucer is so revered by book historians that there is even a recent published census of the existing copies (Oak Knoll Press, 2011), an honor otherwise reserved for the Gutenberg Bible and the first folio of Shakespeare's plays. Morris reverse-engineered an incunabulum (the label given to books published in the first fifty years of the era of print in the West) as an act of peaceful defiance of authority. At a time when other forces in book production were pushing for cheaper substrates, faster production and consumption, more convenience, and greater portability, Morris's rejection of every one of these trends was a considered act of text technological subversion. Morris chose for his landmark edition the author he considered the father of English literature to strengthen the notion that this text could in some way catalyze a rebirth of literary culture and stimulate a return to authenticity and soulfulness.

This text's aura and its intentionality overlap considerably, but its functionality is, sadly, slightly different. Copies now routinely sell for between $75,000 and $250,000. While the Kelmscott Chaucer is a statement about the profound dignity that work can have, that work was possible under very particular, rather unusual (and materially unconstrained) circumstances. In fact, Morris's edition of Chaucer took a loss even though it was fully subscribed before printing began. As a manifesto for the reinvention of our patterns of consumption, it is a poignant failure and failed experiment. In fact, the self-consciousness of this text's aura finally undermines its functionality.

PART 4   TRANSFORMATIONS

IN PART 4, we look at one aspect of text technologies that we have so far mentioned only in passing: the process by which one technology gives rise to, or gives way to, another. The shift from one text technology to another often reveals much about the functions, materials, and intentions of each, as well as the capacities and desires of users to integrate those factors into their lives. In short, the transformation from one text technology to another can reveal newly apparent shortcomings in an older technology that the newer technology remedies. Often that newer technology will turn out to have shortcomings that its earliest designers could never have conceived of, and when that turns out to be the case, the cycle begins again, and a new text technology will supplant it.

As you read Part 4, which contains discussions of the transition from manuscript to print, from scroll to codex, and from CD to mp3, think about the technologies in your own life and consider which ones you think might be vulnerable to being replaced by something better tailored to the conditions of your existence. If there is something that you think is likely, ask yourself, Why hasn't it happened yet? What is holding it back?

MANUSCRIPT TO PRINT
In the West, the text technological transition from manuscript to print is one of the most significant events of the past thousand years. The

impact of that transition is the subject of many books and articles, and here we trace only some of its most significant aspects.[1] The simplest way to describe the movement from manuscript to print is as a media shift or a communications shift: when we talk about a text technological transformation, we talk about how new ways of conveying meaning were driven by, and themselves drove, social change. To discuss a text technological transformation is to ask how changes of tool and substrate and innovations in production, transmission, and consumption both created new arenas of social possibility and were created to occupy those arenas.

One of the most visible changes wrought by the advent of print was the vast growth of literacy it made possible. It is often remarked that print made the dissemination of texts much cheaper, but this is true only once a certain numbers of copies have been made. There is a simple economic logic behind this fact: the more texts a printer produced, the lower the marginal cost of producing another became. The result was the economic possibility of a far greater number of texts that could be produced than under the old method of large-scale production, the scriptorium or writing office. A scriptorium could produce texts faster than lone scribes, but the net cost of producing books in a scriptorium was usually higher than the sunk cost of setting a text in movable type and printing it once the sunk cost of setting the text was met.[2]

As the graphs on the next page show, the initial cost of producing texts in a printing press (left) is higher than the initial cost in a scriptorium (right). But as the number of texts produced increases, the printing press becomes significantly cheaper than the scriptorium, which incurs only minimal savings through collaborative production. Print therefore necessitated larger readerships in order to be more economically viable than had manuscript.[3]

The most noted corollary of this point is that print brought a boom in literacy to Europe. But as we will see, print transformed the intellectual lives of highly literate scholars as much as it did those of previously unlettered artisans. The economies of scale, after all, apply equally to rare and expensive books and to cheap broadsheets and handbills. In fact, one might argue that the printing press changed everything. As Sigrid Steinberg writes, "Neither political, constitutional, ecclesiastical,

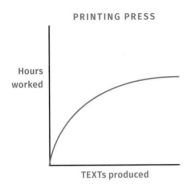

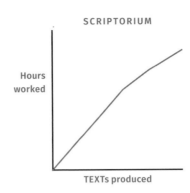

and economic events, nor sociological, philosophical, and literary movements can be fully understood without taking into account the influence the printing press has exerted on them."[4] It is hard to gauge just how transformative the advent of print was because it has entirely reshaped the way that we think about communication, data collection, retention, circulation, and organization. Our very ideas of intellectual categorization and standardization have been shaped first by manuscript technologies and then by the printing press. To examine in depth the transformations the press engendered is to undertake a genealogy of many aspects of modernity.

The first codex printed with movable type in western Europe was Johannes Gutenberg's forty-two-line Bible, discussed in Part 2.[5] Behind this monolithic achievement, however (which we can date to around 1450 or shortly thereafter), there are several distinct innovations:

The development of oil-based inks to replace water-based inks
The adaptation of the agricultural press (like that used for pressing grapes) to press blocks of type
The invention of mass-produced metal movable type

To understand the magnitude of Gutenberg's achievement, it's necessary to understand that any one of these technological innovations alone would have been highly significant. To have made and combined all three is an extraordinary feat. Gutenberg found that water-soluble inks created blurs in the printing process and so developed an oil-based substitute. He created a special alloy (printer's lead) for his metal type and developed a hand mold to make any extra type that the print shop might need on short notice. In short, what we refer to as the invention of printing is actually a constellation of remarkable technological innovations in both substrates and tools.[6] Before Gutenberg adapted agricultural presses for his own model, for example, wine and cheese makers had to invent their own model of a screw press to maximize the yield of their products. Metallurgy had to advance to a point where new alloys were plausible developments. In the same way, Gutenberg made possible later technological innovations: movable metal type was the first kind of mechanical manufacture to rely on a system of replaceable parts, on which principle most of the world's manufacturing proceeds today. So to describe Gutenberg's achievement as something that simply happened one day is to view as one the many convergent technological threads that came together to make that achievement possible.

What the printing press made possible was more remarkable still. Sixty years after the printing of the Gutenberg Bible, when the practice of printing had spread throughout Europe and tens of thousands of titles had been printed, Martin Luther wrote his 95 Theses.[7] Luther's arguments were predicated on the principle that the sacred text of Christianity, the Bible, was something that anyone ought to be able to read and interpret for themselves. In rejecting the authority of the pope on matters like purgatory, Luther symbolically rejected the entire structure of dissemination on which the Catholic Church was founded: learning came from the literate clergy and was then preached to illiterate congregants. The alternative that emerged was a kind of Christianity holding that congregants could read and interpret for themselves: Protestantism. Without printing, however, there would have been barely any literate nonclergy, and therefore no fuel for Luther's fire. This text technological innovation created a new social form; indeed, it precipitated an entire religious schism in Europe.

Printing changed not only the number of people who could read or the number of texts that those people read. It changed reading itself. One could also argue that typography gave letters a more standardized shape for the first time (although medieval scripts were often very formal and themselves quite standard). The roots of typography lie, with much of the rest of the Renaissance, in fourteenth-century Florence, where Niccolò Niccoli and Poggio Bracciolini developed a form of handwriting (called "a hand") that was designed for maximum legibility. They were part of a circle of intellectuals sending and forwarding letters all over the continent, and a standardized hand was crucial for this community of people who might never meet to understand one another.[8] But inevitably hands were still practiced differently by different writers, even if only in minor detail. With metal type, it became much easier to read not only because there were more materials available at a lower cost (though those were indubitably factors), but because letters simply tended to look more alike. New readers had fewer letterforms to learn because they would encounter many times fewer formal variations.

Typefaces were not the only thing that printing regularized. The metal type was set in a frame of a size set to fit the size and format of paper being used. These frames themselves rested on a bed. With regularized sizes of printing beds and frames, margins became far more regular, though, again, manuscript technologies had already included margins, writing grids, ruling, rubrication, and paragraph marks. When we think of data organization or informational retrieval tools, we might not think of units like paragraphs as technologies. But that is exactly the work done by a paragraph, and a regular margin is key to being able to see where a paragraph is. Margins that were always straight and predictable meant that readers who were coming to a text for the very first time could see at a glance the rough organization of ideas on the page.[9] Standardization also transformed the transmission and reliability of word lists, grammars, maps, and (of course) laws.

While printing spread literacy as no other innovation before (and with the possible exception of the internet since), it also revolutionized the work of the most literate scholars and thinkers. Standardization made possible conversations between intellectuals that had never happened before; scholars could correspond with one another knowing as they never had hitherto that they were reading similar texts. And while printing did make possible the dissemination of new texts faster and more cheaply, it also changed the reproduction of old texts. Accepted editions of texts became possible. Because it was cheaper to produce many copies of a text, scholars' ideas could spread further and faster and reach readers relatively unmediated by individual, partial, or illegible transcriptions (whether undertaken in good or bad faith). As the cost of printed books brought the price of knowledge down and poorer scholars could afford more books, synthetic thinking that brought together many threads became more possible for more people. Scholars no longer had to travel the Continent to read a specific text (held only in manuscript in select libraries) or to be well versed in all the arguments made on a single topic; they could go to one major center of learning (such as Paris, Heidelberg, or Geneva) and stay put.

Scholars argue too that the printing press not only remade the word and what could be done with words; it also changed the way Europe consumed images. Many of the same dynamics applied: engraved images could be transmitted more reliably, faster, and much more cheaply than they ever could when made by woodblocks. Protestant propagandists exploited this to a great extent by circulating visual satires on Catholicism.[10] With cheaper and more reliable image reproduction, it became possible to speak to the nonliterate more clearly and more widely than it ever had been before. Accordingly, even though Protestantism was a phenomenon born of increased literacy, Protestant satirists could use the same mechanism that had given rise to their cause to address even illiterate people.

Printing enabled amplified cross-continental ideological cohesion among large groups of people. Phenomena like the Republic of Letters, the Scientific Revolution, and the foundation of modern systems of finance all owed their very possibility to the printing press. Ultimately, the technological innovations of the printing press are important because they are not bound by their very first substrate and tools. The term *print culture* is used to describe the intellectual and social forms that arose after Gutenberg. This is the legacy of the printing press: the supersession of outdated substrates has not changed our ways of making, transmitting, or consuming information or our overarching categories of information. Whether the majority of the texts that we read today are printed on handpresses, or on modern presses, or whether they are in fact never printed at all, our culture is, in its organizing principles, a print culture. Nevertheless, it should be borne in mind that with our notebooks and pens, manuscript technology is more common and widely used than ever before.

COMPACT DISC TO MP3

The shift in dominance from the compact disc (CD) to the mp3 (moving picture experts group audio layer III) is slow and ongoing. The two technologies have fundamentally different intentions, and the materiality of each has been designed to serve those intentions. The gradual replacement of CDs with mp3s is a function of how we use recorded sound. We will survey the material and technological differences between the two formats in this section before suggesting the motivating factors behind the change.

Despite its name, the CD was not a text technology optimized for compactness and portability. The CD is "compact" only by comparison with its much larger forerunner, the 12-inch LaserDisc, the technology's first iteration, using the same reading tool (a 780-nanometer-wavelength semiconductor laser) and the same substrate.[11] The 4.7-inch CD was optimized for verisimilitude of reproduction. The technology of digitally encoding audio data onto an extremely thin sheet of aluminum adhered to a transparent plastic disc was jointly pioneered by technicians at Sony and Philips.[12]

The playing time for a CD is eighty minutes; the earliest CDs had a playing time of seventy-four minutes. One rumored explanation for this storage capacity is that a Sony executive wanted the format to be able to contain Wilhelm Furtwangler's seminal 1951 recording of Beethoven's Ninth Symphony. Another is that the diameter of the CD was made to be the same length as the hypotenuse of a compact cassette tape. Whatever the case, the compact disc was a remarkable improvement over previous audio technology; it could contain almost four times as much information as a vinyl disc. The capacity of the previous high-fidelity technology, the long-playing 33 rpm vinyl disc, was twenty-two minutes per side.

Indeed, the CD offered multiple innovations. By replacing the needle used with the vinyl disc with a mechanically operated laser, it became possible not only to skip perfectly between tracks but to skip within a track at a reliable speed without ever risking damage to the substrate.[13] Like its predecessor, the CD comes with packaging. The jewel case holds the CD in a protective cradle, and the creator or distributor of the TEXT can include a printed sleeve. The inclusion of liner notes in CD packaging is a sedimented technology from vinyl's sleeves, which were large enough to carry substantial amounts of printed text if desired.

The true functionality of the CD is audio fidelity. CDs are able to store audio data at 1,411.2 kilobits per second (kbps, 1.4 megabits per second of audio playback). By comparison, the highest standard bit rate offered by mp3s is 320 kbps. While the size of the CD was a matter of debate among engineers and executives, the size of the substrate would not have changed the medium's fidelity of reproduction, only the quantity of text that the substrate could hold. The CD is what is called a lossless format because it conveys all data, bar none, encoded in the master recording.

While the functionality of the mp3 is hybrid, more than any other audio format in the history of recorded sound, its key goal is transmissibility. It is not technically correct to speak of an mp3 file as immaterial, since all digital files have their material instantiations on hard discs as sequences of electromagnetic signals. But an mp3 file can be dematerialized, rematerialized, moved, or duplicated without any corruption of the text. In this sense, the CD is an analog substrate, even while the data on a CD are digitally encoded.

The emphasis on transmissibility has profound consequences for the mp3. The smaller a file is, the faster it can be transmitted and the more files a user is able to store and access. Therefore, the mp3 is designed to be as small as possible. It is often 12 percent of the size of the same file encoded onto a CD. To do this, an mp3 is compressed in two ways.

The more important, innovative, and substantial compression method draws on the insights of psychoacoustics, the study of sound as a perceptual event (rather than as a purely physical phenomenon). Because the perceptual mechanisms of the ear and brain are attuned to certain frequencies rather than others, mp3 encoding can safely remove data that a perceptual modeling algorithm judges to be imperceptible. For example, the upper end of human hearing is around a frequency of 20 kilohertz (kHz). As humans age, this upper limit drops to around 16 kHz. But the brain is adapted to be most sensitive to frequencies in the range of 2 to 4 kHz, the range occupied by the human voice, so the designer of an mp3's encoding algorithm can assign it to remove data in the 16 to 20 kHz range in the knowledge that this loss of data will not be correspondingly perceived by a listener, who has evolved to focus on lower-frequency sounds. This is known as perceptual compression. A CD, by contrast, encodes all auditory data regardless of a listener's potential perceptual limits. The second compression method mp3 coders use is much simpler: an mp3 encoding algorithm will search for and remove repetitive or redundant data.

The result is that we have two technologies with two different goals: one is made to produce perfect sounds, the other to sound good enough while giving the illusion of immateriality. So why should the mp3 win out over the CD? The answer has to do with how we listen to sound, whether spoken word or music. The popularity of the mp3 format has been fueled by, and has fueled, our expectation that music can be present in our lives whether we are driving, jogging, working, at a party, drinking, shopping, or going to sleep. In the majority of these cases, we bring our music with us, which means portability is a key concern, so the mp3's apparent immateriality is essential. We want to have the widest choice of sounds possible available to us in the least physically noticeable way possible. But the corollary to this is that in those circumstances, we are not actively listening to sound; rather, we are hearing it, noticing it surrounding us, being comforted by the insulation it provides us.

When was the last time you sat down to listen to music and do nothing else? Rhythms, tunes, words, and even complex harmonies will survive severe signal degradation without our noticing, in large part because most of us don't care to notice. The idea of sound quality is, if not alien, largely irrelevant. When we instrumentalize sound, we listen to it to hear that it is there. The popularity of the mp3 crystallizes a basic truth about contemporary consumers of audio texts: the fact of an audio text's existence is more important to most consumers than its quality.

Some commentators have expressed bafflement that with the popularization of the mp3, the direction of "progress" appears to be toward lesser verisimilitude; indeed, similar arguments have been made about digital cameras as compared to their analog predecessors. But technological innovation is not driven by the pursuit of abstract ideals like verisimilitude, purity, or the presence of the ideal conditions for aesthetic contemplation. Socially constructive technological innovation responds to demand created by new social practices: if users want to consume a text under certain conditions (going for a run, or even while swimming), then innovation will respond to that demand to make it possible with new substrates and tools. Indeed, to speak of progress in text technological change is a way to attach value to a value-neutral phenomenon. The idea that progress corresponds only to the search for ever more perfect verisimilitude is produced by conservative anxiety about the gap between intentionality and functionality. As we saw in Part I in the section on sedimentation, because texts are so social, less flexible users of texts are made uncomfortable by users who apply their own functionalities to texts and text technologies.

The advent of the mp3 has allowed a tremendous flowering of functionalities for the underlying texts. As much as transmissibility, the intentionality of the mp3 is also vastly flexible functionality. No matter how convenient portable CD players became, the materiality of CD technology was always geared toward a value that users no longer cared about. In the slow demise of the CD and concomitant rise of the mp3, we can see the technological reflection of the way that audio texts are used now.

SCROLL TO CODEX

The scroll is a text technology that allows producers to store texts of almost any length in one place. Usually made by joining together many separate leaves made of the same material, the scroll offers convenience of storage, access, and portability as compared to multiple individual leaves. The scroll is usually formed of a long strip of folios or leaves with a wooden roller attached to each end. In its closed form, the scroll is essentially cylindrical. To use the scroll, the user unrolls it to make a portion of text visible. As substrate unrolls from one roller, it is wound onto the other. Because the scroll is a single, apparently continuous physical object, it offered its users the ability to impose a linear order on separate documents. Scrolls of parchment or paper were editable as well as portable; more than ever before, a text, or multiple texts, could be moved around, amended, continuously written, expanded, erased, and rewritten. So given this great flexibility, it's interesting to consider why the scroll lost out to the technology of the codex.

The codex is a rectilinear object consisting of a series of regularly shaped folios bound together. Like the scroll, those substrates can be parchment or paper (or even a small number of conjoined wax tablets). To travel with a scroll and protect it from rain, sunlight, sand, and dirt, users had to put it in a case. This meant that in practice, the scroll was rather bulkier to carry around in a way that ensured the text's long-term survival. One of the innovations of the bound codex was that the technology of binding incorporated the function of the scroll case in such a way that the substrates were always covered and protected.

But the reason that the codex and the binding basically replaced scroll technology goes deeper than simply ensuring the protection of their substrates from accident. Perhaps most significant, the folios of the codex can be inscribed on both sides; in the case of the scroll, writing generally can be inscribed only on one side of the substrate. As such, it is possible to make much better use of the substrate when it is cut into leaves and bound into codex form. This fact had important economic implications, for twice as much information could be stored in a codex as on a scroll with a similar number of leaves.

Moreover, to open a scroll takes two hands: one to unroll from the direction of unread material and one to roll up the read material. One has to then carefully retain the right amount of tension between the two rollers, enough for the scroll to be static and legible but not so taut as to endanger the substrate. To write on a scroll takes more. First, the roll has to be unrolled to the desired place and then placed on a hard surface that will support the use of a writing tool. In practice, the scroll needs to be held open with at least one and possibly two weights to keep it from rolling itself up. The longer the scroll is kept rolled up, the more the substrate will become warped into the shape of a spiral. To write on a scroll, then, takes an apparatus of solid surface and weights.

The codex is basically hand-shaped. This means that it can be opened with one hand and kept open with one hand. The binding of the codex incorporates the solid surface needed for tool use. If you choose to put the codex on a surface to write on it, it will (sometimes) hold itself open without any aids. Under those circumstances, all a text producer needs to write in a codex is a suitable tool.

None of these innovations, however, was truly transformative. What really made the difference in the codex's favor was the completely new way it offered users to access content. The scroll's great strength lay in its ability to string together multiple texts into one longer linear text. But that strength was also a weakness: once the scroll had been assembled, there was no way to access those texts other than by scrolling through the substrate until the section required was found. The codex's innovation is simple: with a series of bound folios, it is equally fast to access any single section of material. Rather than being bound to the structure of the scroll, users can open the codex at any point they choose, close it, and then reopen it at any other point. This is absolutely impossible for a scroll and allows much faster and more efficient access to the content inscribed on the substrate.

The codex allows other, related innovations. The most successful text technologies take full advantage of the ways in which we experience them. Scrolls are made to be moved by hands. Though we use our hands to move through a codex, the most important way we interact with a codex is with our fingers, to pick up, turn, leaf through, fold, or tear pages. Because we have so many fingers, we can easily mark our place in a codex with one finger, consult another place in the codex, even a third, and then return to the first place, all while holding the codex. This kind of comparative work was impossible on a scroll without the use of a very long table or floor to expose two distant sections simultaneously.

This has a very important consequence for information organization. The codex makes any kind of nonlinear information organization into a material possibility. One could even argue that the codex's emphasis on the possibility of atomized content enabled the very concept of information as an excerptible, decontextualizable fact. The chapter (originally *capitulum*, or head) did exist as a rubric for information organization in the scroll; the rubric itself was written in red ink (from Latin *rubus*, meaning red). But the organization of those headings was still bound by the physical configuration of the substrate. What the codex made fully possible was a nonsubsidiary arrangement of conceptual material. With separate leaves comes the possibility of separate sections. Discrete sections of a codex can advance arguments that are different, related, or consequent to one another—at the text producer's discretion. With the release from strictly linear writing, it becomes far easier to make wider intellectual connections and gather together more disparate threads into deeper and more unexpected syntheses. The codex truly permitted a new kind of thinking for text producers, as well as more flexible reading for consumers. It may have made possible the very idea of reference, of data and arguments rather than single monolithic narratives. The intellectual formations that the codex enables are far more powerful as transformative factors than pragmatic considerations about fingers and hands: the production of texts with an intention that demands a certain material configuration is a more powerful engine of technological change than convenience or inconvenience.

Until relatively recently, this was the end of the contest between the scroll and the codex. In the past twenty-five years, however, the scroll has come back. Most websites now incorporate the scroll into the page. Facebook's news feed is (currently) an infinitely unfurling scroll, as is a Twitter time line. Websites often contain multiple scrolling options catalogued under different pages. And this reflects the way that their users engage with them. Scrollable pages now, like their ancestors, are inimical to indexicality and instrumentality: they are designed specifically to be perused at leisure rather than consulted for information. As a rule of thumb, the ratio of scrolls to pages in a website reflects the degree to which that website is designed to be used at the user's leisure rather than for the purposive act of information retrieval. The more a website is designed for pleasure, the more likely it is to have scrollable content on every page, and so the more that ratio will approach 1:1. Conversely, the more static pages a website has (neither dynamic nor scrolling), the more likely it is the site is designed to maximize the indexed storage and discovery of information. On occasion throughout this book we have referred to the *Oxford English Dictionary*'s website. On that site, the only regular changes are filed under "Word of the Day" and "What's New." Otherwise the gap between the second and third editions was about twenty years—not very dynamic but a model of indexicality. The digitized scroll, as embodied in the scroll bar, is an ingenious compromise between the linearity of the scroll and the indexicality of the page (although one might argue that the screen provides a page-like organization, even as one scrolls through a website): it allows users to pick up scrolling wherever they choose in a text. Freed from the constraints that the material scroll placed on users, digital scrolls allow texts to take advantage once again of the uninterrupted surface a scroll offers. The infinitely extensible surface of a dynamic scroll can be more absorbing than any text that relies on turning pages, and this can lend a certain cohesion to a text. But however enjoyable the digitally scrollable text might be now, the innovation of the codex permitted epochal transformations in our structures of thought.

The printing press changed completely the speed at which information traveled, its reliability, its affordability, and so on. Faster, cheaper, more: these are comparatives. The printing press brought utterly profound changes, but many of them were of a quantitative character. The transformation wrought by the innovation of the codex, however, was of a different order: it may have made an absolute, qualitative difference to the way users were able to think.

NOTES

PART 1: CONCEPTUAL FRAMEWORK

1. A note on typography: throughout this book, you will often see the word TEXT written in small capitals. This is a technique taken from semantics, where capitals are used to denote a specific high-level term with a subset of subordinate terms (e.g., FURNITURE = chair, table, wardrobe, bed), rather than an ordinary lexical or syntactic unit (i.e., "text"), whose meanings are context dependent. That is, we are treating TEXT as representing the superordinate of the semantic field of all textual production, all text technologies, all writing systems, and all forms of meaningful communication. It is thus the abstraction of all individual instantiations of textual production or TEXT.

2. To an extent we are following Immanuel Kant, who writes in the *Critique of Judgment* that art "is a way of presenting that is purposive on its own and that furthers, even though without a purpose, the culture of our mental powers to [facilitate] social communication." *Critique of Judgment*, trans. Werner S. Pluhar (Indianapolis: Hackett, 1987), 173. Kant's use of the word *communication* is key, since it implies the transmission of information from one agent to one or more others. It follows from our definition of TEXT that we are distinctly anthropocentric in our treatment of text technologies. Our definition of meaning therefore excludes nonhuman or theological sources as being beyond our purview. To an extent, this is an arbitrary hard stop. There are many kinds of nonhuman text. The pheromone trails left by ants to indicate the existence of food and also encode its distance and direction are only one example. Bowerbirds construct elaborate nests according to a set of aesthetic principles; these nests are part of a highly developed set of courtship rituals. It would be utterly fruitless to deny that the pheromonal trails left by ants, the nests of bowerbirds, the dances of birds of paradise, the howls of wolves, or the struts of peacocks were text. And

this is to say nothing of the capacity of gorillas to fashion texts legible across species boundaries. The nonhuman animals we have listed voluntarily and intentionally create perceptible phenomena in order to convey meaning to another agent. Many animals, bees and elephants, for example, use text not only for communication but also (leveraging authority) for social organization. A complete taxonomy of all uses of TEXT across all human and nonhuman agents requires more space than we can afford it here. For the purposes of the taxonomy that this book will establish, therefore, we limit ourselves solely to human-created TEXT.

3. This distinction we also draw from Kant, from his *Critique of Pure Reason*, ed. Paul Guyer and Allen W. Wood (Cambridge: Cambridge University Press, 1999).

4. Earlier investigations of plenitext can be found in Elaine Treharne, "The Architextuality Editing of Old English," *Poetica* 71 (2008): 1–13, and "Fleshing Out the Text: The Transcendent Manuscript in the Digital Age," *Postmedieval* 4 (2013): 465–78.

5. Walter Benjamin, "The Work of Art in the Age of Mechanical Reproduction," in *Illuminations: Essays and Reflections*, trans. Harry Zohn, ed. Hannah Arendt (New York: Schocken / Random House, 2007), 221 (emphasis added).

6. Plato, *Phaedrus*, in *Plato in Twelve Volumes*, vol. 9, trans. Harold N. Fowler (Cambridge, MA: Harvard University Press, 1925), 274–75, sec. 274c–275e.

7. The *Oxford English Dictionary* offers this definition for manufacture (v): "To make (a product, goods, etc.) from, (out) of raw material; to produce (goods) by physical labour, machinery, etc." The *OED* gives the etymology of the word *manufacture* as the ablative of Latin *manus* (by hand) and the Middle French *facture* (the action or process of making [a thing]). We find the presence of the Latin for *hand* in the word *manufacture*—a powerful reminder of the physical, bodily labor of making a text technology (s.v. "manufacture, v," "manufacture, n," and "facture, n." *OED Online*, June 2014. Web. 20 August 2014: http://www.oed.com/.

PART 2: HISTORICAL FRAMEWORK

1. Look up the Law Code of Hammurabi from 1780 BCE and the host stele for a particularly remarkable instance of tablet making.

2. Phonographic alphabets represent units of sound—phonemes—in regularly occurring clusters of written symbols—graphemes. Phonographic and pictographic modes are combined in cuneiform.

3. Classicist R. S. Bagnall has cataloged these fragments in *The Florida Ostraka: Documents from the Roman Army in Upper Egypt*, Greek, Roman, and Byzantine Monographs 7, nos. 1–31 (Durham, NC, 1976).

4. We do not endorse any of these corporate mediaspheres. We discuss them only as examples of a larger phenomenon. Many, many such tables could be constructed.

PART 3: CASE STUDIES

1. The use of Washington may have been, in 1869, a rhetorical harkening back to the founding of the nation and thus, implicitly, a call for unity. By 2014, however, having Washington's face on the dollar bill has a different significance: it is a distinctly democratic perversity to have one of the greatest presidents on the smallest of bills. This is one example of the shift between intentionality (historical design) and functionality (present working).

2. Disk Concept, Rosetta Project, August 23, 2014, http://rosettaproject.org /disk/concept/.

3. It can be seen on the British Museum website: http://www.britishmuseum. org/research/collection_online/collection_object_details.aspx?objectId=32 7188&partId=1.

4. "Cyrus Cylinder," trans. Shahrokh Razmjou and Irving Finkel, British Museum, line 23, http://www.britishmuseum.org/research/collection_online /collection_object_details.aspx?objectId=327188&partId=1.

5. The night that Cyrus took Babylon, Belshazzar was feasting, and a hand wrote on the wall "Mene, mene, tekel upharsim" (Thou art weighed in the balance and found wanting). It is a neat symmetry of history that this act of writing on the wall happens at almost the same moment in time as the creation of the cylinder, one of the best-known pieces of writing in clay.

6. Shapour Ghasemi, "The Cyrus the Great Cylinder," Iran Chamber Society, http://www.iranchamber.com/history/cyrus/cyrus_charter.php.

7. "Shirin Ebadi—Nobel Lecture," Nobelprize.org, December 10, 2013, http://www.nobelprize.org/nobel_prizes/peace/laureates/2003/ebadi-lecture -e.html.

8. TeamRock, "The Story behind the Eagles' Hotel California Album." November 13, 2016, http://teamrock.com/feature/2016-11-13/the-story-behind -the-eagles-hotel-california-album-artwork-interview.

9. Don Henley in Rolling Stone, April 7, 2011, https://www.rollingstone .com/music/lists/the-500-greatest-songs-of-all-time-20110407/the-eagles-hotel -california-20110525.

10. William Morris, cited in "The Kelmscott Chaucer," http://www.bl.uk /onlinegallery/onlineex/landprint/kelmscott/.

11. Robert Milevski, "The Kelmscott Press Chaucer, and the Princeton University Library," Princeton University Library Rare Books Collection Blog, 2005 [pubd 2011], http://blogs.princeton.edu/rarebooks/docs/Milevski_PUL_Kelm- scott_Article.pdf .

12. It is important to record the contributions of R. Catterson-Smith and William Harcourt Hooper, who painted over and then engraved Burne-Jones's images, respectively.

PART 4: TRANSFORMATIONS

1. The key and foundational work on this topic is Elizabeth Eisenstein's *The Printing Press as an Agent of Change*, vols. 1 and 2 (Cambridge: Cambridge University Press, 1979). Marshall McLuhan's *The Gutenberg Galaxy* (Toronto: University of Toronto Press, 1962) offers a more symptomatic overview of the transformations wrought by print, whereas Eisenstein attempts a more comprehensive survey of the causes, mechanics, and consequences of the transition from manuscript to print from 1400 to 1700, largely as seen in western Europe. The work of Walter J. Ong also offers seminal articulations of the conceptual shift brought about by print. Philip Gaskell, *A New Introduction to Bibliography* (New Castle, DE: Oak Knoll, 2000) and Fredson Bowers, *Principles of Bibliographic Description* (New Castle, DE: Oak Knolll, 2012) have written the two most complete anatomies of the composition of the early modern and modern printed book.

2. Of course, the story of the evolving production of texts between, say, 1200 and 1500 was far more complex than "first scriptoria, then print shops," but we employ the changeover here as a convenient fiction.

3. This trend continues today. Publishers would rather print a smaller number of better-selling books than a larger number of modest-selling books. In Britain, publishers sell more units than ever before, but those units comprise fewer separate texts.

4. Sigfrid H. Steinberg, *Five Hundred Years of Printing* (London: Penguin Books, 1961), 11, citing Eisenstein, *The Printing Press as an Agent of Change*, 7.

5. The world's first movable type (made of wood, and later porcelain) was pioneered in China in the eleventh century. Comprehensive accounts of the origins of movable type printing also include Johannes Fust, Peter Schoeffer, and Laurens Coster (whom some regard as having "invented printing" slightly before Gutenberg).

6. Other social innovations created the conditions that made those innovations possible. Gutenberg was able to secure investments from figures we would now call venture capitalists and took out many loans. He also ran an organized and bureaucratized workforce. Without these social forms, his inventions would never have been conceivable, let alone executable.

7. Eisenstein writes in *The Printing Press as an Agent of Change* (44), "Unknown anywhere in Europe before the mid-fifteenth century, printers' workshops would be found in every important metropolitan center by 1500."

8. For more on the development of roman and italic scripts, see Martin Davies, "Humanism in Script and Print in the Fifteenth Century," in *The Cambridge Companion to Renaissance Humanism*, ed. Jill Kraye, 47–62 (Cambridge: Cambridge University Press, 2003).

9. Here we are following Ong's *Ramus, Method, and the Decay of Dialogue* (Chicago: University of Chicago Press, 1954) and "System, Space, and Intellect in Renaissance Symbolism," *Bibliothèque d'humanisme et Renaissance* 18 (1956): 222–39. Ong argued that Peter Ramus, a Renaissance pedagogue, dovetailed his argumentative structures with the material structures of print to enhance the persuasiveness of his writing.

10. See this image, for example: http://www.metmuseum.org/toah/images /hb/hb_53.677.5.jpg.

11. The LaserDisc's substrate was unencoded and thus analog, but the actual method of recording information, a spiral series of very small impressions and bumps, was the same as the CD.

12. One consequence of the collaborative corporate partnership that produced the CD format was that the two companies released a volume, *The Red Book*, with precise specifications for CDs. The standard for mp3s is de facto rather than de jure and is defined in ISO/IEC-11172-3. The best study of the mp3 format as a whole is Jonathan Sterne's *Mp3: The Meaning of a Format* (Durham, NC: Duke University Press, 2012).

13. It is a major weakness of the vinyl disc and needle as a substrate/tool pair that an incorrectly used needle can permanently damage a vinyl disc.

BIBLIOGRAPHY

Some of the entries that follow are additional to those cited in the main text. It is also worthwhile to consult bibliographies on book history and on the history of information and media, especially of cultures globally, and languages other than English.

Abadia, Oscar Moro, and Manuel R. Morales Gonzalez. "Thinking about 'Style' in the 'Post-Stylistic Era': Reconstructing the Stylistic Context of Chauvet." *Oxford Journal of Archaeology* 26 (2007): 109–25.

Abramson, Albert. *The History of Television, 1942 to 2000.* Jefferson, NC: McFarland, 2003.

Addison, Joseph. "'Introducing Mr. Spectator.'" March 1, 1711. The Spectator Project @ Rutgers. http://bit.ly/148JFHK.

Adorno, Theodore. *Essays on Music.* Berkeley: University of California Press, 2002.

Adorno, Theodore, and Max Horkheimer. *The Dialectic of Enlightenment.* Stanford, CA: Stanford University Press, 2002.

Allen, Alistair. *The History of Printed Scraps.* London: New Cavendish Books, 1983.

Andrews, Carol. *The Rosetta Stone.* London: British Museum Press, 1981.

Angeletti, Norberto, and Alberto Oliva. *Magazines That Make History: Their Origins, Development, and Influence.* Gainesville: University Press of Florida, 2004.

Althusser, Louis. "Ideology and Ideological State Apparatuses." *La Pensée 150* (1970): 3–38.

Altick, Richard D. *The English Common Reader: A Social History of the Mass Reading Public.* Chicago: University of Chicago Press, 1957.

———. "Nineteenth-Century English Periodicals." *Newberry Library Bulletin* 9 (1952): 255–64.

Attali, Jacques. *Noise: The Political Economy of Music.* Minneapolis: University of Minnesota Press, 1985.

Austin, Joe. *Taking the Train: How Graffiti Art Became an Urban Crisis in New York City.* New York: Columbia University Press, 2002.

Avrin, L. *Scribes, Script and Books.* London: British Library, 1991.

Baghoolizadeh, Bheeta. "Reconstructing a Persian Past: Contemporary Uses and Misuses of the Cyrus Cylinder in Iranian Nationalist Discourse." AjamMC.com. http://bit.ly/14uchSZ.

Bagnall, Roger S. *The Florida Ostraka: Documents from the Roman Army in Upper Egypt.* Durham, NC: Duke University Press, 1976.

———. *Hellenistic and Roman Egypt: Sources and Approaches.* Aldershot, UK: Ashgate, 2006.

Baikie, James. *Egyptian Papyri and Papyrus-Hunting.* New York: Kessinger, 1926.

Barthes, Roland. "The Death of the Author." In *Image, Music, Text*, translated by S. Heath, 142–48. London: Fontana, 1977.

Bartlett, Jamie. *The Dark Net: Inside the Digital Underworld.* London: William Heinemann, 2014.

Beaulieu, Paul-Alain. "An Episode in the Fall of Babylon to the Persians." *Journal of Near Eastern Studies* 52 (1993): 241–61.

Beegan, Gerry. *The Mass Image: A Social History of Photomechanical Reproduction in Victorian London.* Basingstoke, UK: Palgrave Macmillan, 2008.

Benjamin, Walter. "Theses on the Philosophy of History." 1940. https://www.marxists.org/reference/archive/benjamin/1940/history.htm.

———. "The Work of Art in the Age of Mechanical Reproduction." In *Illuminations: Essays and Reflections*, translated by Harry Zohn, edited by Hannah Arendt. New York: Schocken/Random House, 2007.

Benjamin, Walter, Michael William Jennings, Brigid Doherty, Thomas Y. Levin, and E. F. N. Jephcott. *The Work of Art in the Age of Its Technological Reproducibility, and Other Writings on Media.* Cambridge, MA: Belknap Press of Harvard University Press, 2008.

Berger, John. *Ways of Seeing.* London: BBC and Penguin, 1972.

Berners-Lee, Tim, and Daniel Connolly. "Hypertext Markup Language (HTML): A Representation of Textual Information and Meta Information for Retrieval and Interchange." June 1993. w3.org.

Blair, Ann. "Reading Strategies for Coping with Information Overload ca. 1550–1700." *Journal of the History of Ideas* 64 (2003): 11–28.

Blair, John. "Breamore." In *Blackwell Encyclopaedia of Anglo-Saxon England*, edited by Michael Lapidge, Simon Keynes, and Donald Scragg. Oxford, UK: Blackwell, 1999.

Blanchard, Margaret A., ed. *History of the Mass Media in the United States: An Encyclopedia*. London: Routledge, 1998.

Bland, Mark. "The Appearance of the Text in Early Modern England." *Text* 11 (1999): 91–154.

Bliss, D. P. *A History of Wood-Engraving*, rev. ed. London: British Museum, 1964.

Bloom, Jonathan. *Paper before Print: The History and Impact of Paper in the Islamic World*. New Haven, CT: Yale University Press, 2001.

Bond, Donald F. "The Spectator." *Newberry Library Bulletin* 8 (1952): 239–41.

Bowen, Tracey E. "Graffiti Art: A Contemporary Study of Toronto Artists." *Studies in Art Education* 41 (1999): 22–39.

Bowman, A. K., J. M. Brady, R. S. O. Tomlin, and J. D. Thomas. "A Corpus of Writing-Tablets from Roman Britain." N.d. http://www.csad.ox.ac.uk/rib /ribiv/jp1.htm.

Boynton, Susan, and Diane Reilly, eds. *The Practice of the Bible in the Middle Ages: Production, Reception, and Performance in Western Christianity*. New York: Columbia University Press, 2011.

Branscomb, Anne W. "Common Law for the Electronic Frontier." *Scientific American* 265 (1991): 154–58.

Brantley, Jessica. "The Prehistory of the Book." *PMLA* 124 (2009): 632–39.

Brattin, Joel. *Project Boz: Dickens and Serial Fiction*. 2012. http://dickens.wpi.edu /history.html.

Brooker, Peter, and Andrew Thacker, eds. *The Oxford Critical and Cultural History of Modernist Magazines*. Vol. 1, *Britain and Ireland, 1880–1955*. Oxford: Oxford University Press, 2009.

Brown, Michelle P. "The Role of the Wax Tablet in Medieval Literacy: A Reconsideration in Light of a Recent Find in York." *British Library Journal* 20 (1994): 1–17.

———. "The Triumph of the Codex: The Manuscript Book before 1100." In *Companion to the History of the Book*, edited by Simon Eliot and Jonathan Rose, 179–93. Oxford, UK: Wiley-Blackwell, 2009.

Brown, Michelle P., and Patricia Lovett. *The Historical Source Book for Scribes*. Toronto: University of Toronto Press, 1999.

Brownrigg, Linda L., ed. *Making the Medieval Book: Techniques of Production*. Los Altos Hill, CA: Anderson-Lovelace / Red Gull, 1995.

Brumbaugh, R. S. *The Most Mysterious Manuscript: The Voynich "Roger Bacon" Cipher Manuscript*. Carbondale: Southern Illinois University Press, 1978.

Burch, Noël. *Life to Those Shadows*. London: British Film Institute, 1990.

Burke, Seán. *Authorship, a Reader: From Plato to the Postmodern.* Edinburgh: Edinburgh University Press, 1996.

Campbell, Gordon. *The Bible: The Story of the King James Version.* Oxford: Oxford University Press, 2011.

Caplan, Jane, ed. *Written on the Body: The Tattoo in European and American History.* Princeton, NJ: Princeton University Press, 2000.

Carrière, Jean-Claude, and Umberto Eco. *This Is Not the End of the Book: A Conversation Curated by Jean-Philippe de Tonnac.* London: Vintage, 2012.

Cave, Roderick, and Sara Ayad. *A History of the Book in 100 Books.* London: British Library, 2014.

Chartier, Roger. "Labourers and Voyagers: From the Text to the Reader." *Diacritics* 22, no. 2 (1992): 49–61.

———. *On the Edge of the Cliff: History, Language and Practices.* Baltimore: Johns Hopkins University Press, 1997.

———. *The Order of Books: Readers, Authors, and Libraries in Europe between the Fourteenth and Eighteenth Centuries,* trans. Lydia G. Cochrane. Cambridge, UK: Polity Press, 1994.

Childress, Diana. *Johannes Gutenberg and the Printing Press.* Minneapolis: Twenty-First Century Books, 2008.

Clanchy, M. T. *From Memory to Written Record, 1066–1307,* 3rd ed. Oxford, UK: Wiley-Blackwell, 2012.

———. "Parchment and Paper: Manuscript Culture 1100–1500." In *Companion to the History of the Book,* edited by Simon Eliot and Jonathan Rose, 194–206. Oxford, UK: Wiley-Blackwell, 2009.

Clemens, Ray, ed. *The Voynich Manuscript.* New Haven, CT: Yale University Press, 2016.

Clemens, Ray, and Timothy Graham. *An Introduction to Manuscript Studies.* Ithaca, NY: Cornell University Press, 2007.

Clottes, Jean. "Chauvet Cave (ca. 30,000 B.C.)." In *Heilbrunn Timeline of Art History.* New York: Metropolitan Museum of Art, 2002. http://bit.ly/195Qqzp.

Codecademy. N.d. http://bit.ly/15UGK9F.

Collon, Dominique, ed. *7000 Years of Seals.* London: Trustees of the British Museum, 1997.

Cooley, Alison E. *The Cambridge Manual of Latin Epigraphy.* Cambridge: Cambridge University Press, 2012.

Cormode, Graham. "Key Differences between Web 1.0 and Web 2.0." *First Monday* 13, no. 6 (2008). doi:10.5210/fm.v13i6.2125.

Crick, Julia, and Alexandra Walsham, eds. *The Uses of Script and Print, 1300–1700,* Cambridge: Cambridge University Press, 2004.

Cropper, Mark. *The Leaves We Write On: James Cropper; A History in Paper-Making.* London: Ellergreen Press, 2004.

Culler, Jonathan. *The Pursuit of Signs: Semiotics, Literature, Deconstruction.* Ithaca, NY: Cornell University Press, 1981.

Darnton, Robert. *The Business of Enlightenment: The Publishing History of "The Encyclopédie," 1775–1800.* Cambridge, MA: Harvard University Press, 1979.

———. "What Is the History of Books?" *Daedalus* 111, no. 3 (1982): 65–83.

———. "'What Is the History of Books?' Revisited." *Modern Intellectual History* 4, no. 3 (2007): 495–508.

Da Rold, Orietta. "Materials." In The *Production of Books in England, c.1350–1530,* edited by Alexandra Gillespie and Daniel Wakelin, 12–33. Cambridge: Cambridge University Press, 2011.

Da Rold, Orietta, and Elaine Treharne, eds. *Textual Cultures: Cultural Texts: Essays and Studies.* Woodbridge, UK: D. S. Brewer, 2010.

Davies, Martin. "Humanism in Script and Print in the Fifteenth Century." In *The Cambridge Companion to Renaissance Humanism,* edited by Jill Kraye, 47–62. Cambridge: Cambridge University Press, 2003.

Day, Alan. *Inside the British Library.* London: Library Association, 1998.

de Hamel, Christopher. *The Book: A History of the Bible.* London: Phaidon Press, 2001.

———. *Meetings with Remarkable Manuscripts.* London: Allen Lane, 2016.

DeMaria, Robert. *Johnson's Dictionary and the Language of Learning.* Chapel Hill: University of North Carolina Press, 1986.

Derrida, Jacques. *Dissemination.* Translated by Barbara Johnson. Chicago: University of Chicago Press, 1983.

———. *Limited, Inc.* Evanston, IL: Northwestern University Press, 1988.

Derrida, Jacques, and Eric Prenowitz. "Archive Fever: A Freudian Impression." *Diacritics* 25, no. 2 (1995): 9–63.

Doss, Erika. "Spontaneous Memorials and Contemporary Modes of Mourning in America." *Material Religion* 2 (2006): 294–319.

Du Boulay-Hill, A. "A Saxon Church at Breamore, Hants." *Archaeological Journal* 55 (1898): 84–87.

Echard, Sian. "House Arrest: Modern Archives, Medieval Manuscripts." *Journal of Medieval and Early Modern Studies* 30 (2000): 185–210.

Egan, Ronald. "To Count Grains of Sand on the Ocean Floor: Changing Perceptions of Books and Learning in Song Dynasty China." In *Knowledge and Text Production in an Age of Print: China, 900–1400,* edited by Lucille Chia and Hilde De Weerdt, 33–62. Leiden: Brill, 2001.

Eisenstein, Elizabeth. *The Printing Press as an Agent of Change: Communications and Cultural Transformations in Early-Modern Europe*. Cambridge: Cambridge University Press, 1979.

———. *The Printing Revolution in Early Modern Europe*, 2nd rev. ed. Cambridge: Cambridge University Press, 2005.

Elfenbein, Andrew. "Cognitive Science and the History of Reading." *PMLA* 121 (2006): 484–502.

Eliot, Simon, and Jonathan Rose, eds. *Blackwell Companion to the History of the Book*. Oxford: Wiley-Blackwell, 2007.

Emerson, Lori. *Reading Writing Interfaces: From the Digital to the Bookbound*. Minneapolis: University of Minnesota Press, 2014.

Emery, Michael, Edwin Emery, and Nancy L. Roberts. *The Press and America: An Interpretive History of the Mass Media*, 9th ed. Boston: Allyn and Bacon, 1999.

Espejo, Carmen. "European Communication Networks in the Early Modern Age: A New Framework of Interpretation for the Birth of Journalism." *Media History* 17 (2011): 189–202.

Febvre, Henri, and Henri-Jean Martin. *The Coming of the Book: The Impact of Printing, 1450–1800*. London: Verso, 1997.

Federal Communications Commission. "A Short History of Radio: With an Inside Focus on Mobile Radio." Winter 2003–4.

Finkel, I. L., and M. J. Seymour, eds. *Babylon*. Oxford: Oxford University Press, 2009.

Fisher, David E., and Marshall J. Fisher. *Tube: The Invention of Television*. Washington, DC: Counterpoint, 1996.

Fitzpatrick, Kathleen. *Planned Obsolescence: Publishing, Technology, and the Future of the Academy*. New York: New York University Press, 2011.

Fortmueller, Kate. "Arrival of a Train." N.d. *Critical Commons*. http://www .criticalcommons.org/Members/kfortmueller/clips/arrival-of-a-train-aka -l2019arrivee-d2019un-train.

Foucault, Michel. "What Is an Author?" In *Textual Strategies: Perspectives in Post-Structuralist Criticism*, edited by Josué V. Harari, 141–60. Ithaca, NY: Cornell University Press, 1979.

Foys, Martin, and Shannon Bradshaw. 'Developing Digital Mappaemundi: An Agile Mode for Annotating Medieval Maps." *Digital Medievalist* 7 (2011). http://www.digitalmedievalist.org/journal/7/foys/.

Frith, Simon. *Taking Popular Music Seriously*. Aldershot, UK: Ashgate, 2007.

Gameson, Fiona, and Richard Gameson. "The Anglo-Saxon Inscription at St Mary's Church, Breamore, Hampshire." *Anglo-Saxon Studies in Archaeology and History* 6 (1993): 1–10.

Gaskell, Philip. *A New Introduction to Bibliography*. New Castle, DE: Oak Knoll, 2000.

Gaskell, Roger. "Printing House and Engraving Shop." *Book Collector* 53 (2004): 213–51.

Genette, Gerard. "Introduction." In *Paratexts: Thresholds of Interpretation*, translated by Jane E. Lewin, 1–15. Cambridge: Cambridge University Press, 1997.

Gerbner, George. "Mass Media and Human Communication Theory." In *Human Communication Theory*, edited by Frank E. X. Dance, 40–57. New York: Holt, Rinehart and Winston, 1967.

Gillespie, Alexandra. "Analytical Survey: The History of the Book." *New Medieval Literatures* 9 (2007): 245–86.

Gillespie, Alexandra, and Daniel Wakelin, eds. *Production of Books in England, 1350–1500*. Cambridge: Cambridge University Press, 2011.

Gitelman, Lisa. *Paper Knowledge: Toward a Media History of Documents*. Durham, NC: Duke University Press, 2014.

Glanz, Dawn. "The Democratic Art: Pictures for a Nineteenth-Century America, Chromolithography, 1840–1900 (Review)." *Winterthur Portfolio* 16 (1981): 96–99.

Goldstone, Lawrence, and Nancy Goldstone. *The Friar and the Cipher: Roger Bacon and the Unsolved Mystery of the Most Unusual Manuscript in the World*. New York: Doubleday, 2005.

Goody, Jack. *The Logic of Writing and the Organization of Society*. Cambridge: Cambridge University Press, 1988.

Greengrass, Mark, and Lorna Hughes, eds. *The Virtual Representation of the Past*. Aldershot, UK: Ashgate, 2008.

Greetham, D. C. *Textual Scholarship: An Introduction*. New York: Routledge, 1994.

Griffiths, Jeremy, and Derek Pearsall, eds. *Book Production and Publishing in Britain, 1375–1475*. Cambridge: Cambridge University Press, 1989.

Harley, J. B. *The History of Cartography*, vol. 1. Chicago: University of Chicago Press, 1992.

Harvey, P. D. A. *Mappa Mundi: The Hereford World Map*. London: British Library Studies in Medieval Culture, 1996.

Harvey, P. D. A., and Andrew McGuinness. *A Guide to British Medieval Seals*. London: British Library and Public Record Office, 1996.

Haveman, Heather A. *Magazines and the Making of America: Modernization, Community, and Print Culture, 1741–1860*. Princeton, NJ: Princeton University Press, 2015.

Hayles, Katherine N. *Writing Machines*. Cambridge, MA: MIT Press, 2002.

Hazanavicius, Michel. *The Artist*. Dir. Michel Hazanavicius. Studio 37, 2012.

Hellinga, Lotte, ed. *Cambridge History of the Book in Britain*. 3 vols. Cambridge, UK: Cambridge University Press, 1999.

Hendler, J. "Web 3.0 Emerging." *Computer* 42 (2009): 111–13.

Hermer, Joe, and Alan Hunt. "Official Graffiti of the Everyday." *Law and Society Review* 30 (1996): 455–80.

Hicks, Marie. *Programmed Inequality: How Britain Discarded Women Technologists and Lost Its Edge in Computing*. Cambridge, MA: MIT Press, 2017.

Hiley, David. *Western Plainchant: A Handbook*. Oxford, UK: Clarendon Press, 1983.

Hind, A. M. *An Introduction to a History of Woodcut*. New York: Dover, 1935; Boston: Houghton Mifflin; repr., 1963.

Hoare, Peter, ed. *The Cambridge History of Libraries in Britain and Ireland*. 3 vols. Cambridge: Cambridge University Press, 2006.

Holland, Peter, and Stephen Orgel, eds. *From Performance to Print in Shakespeare's England*. New York: Palgrave Macmillan, 2008.

Hume, Robert D. "The Aims and Uses of 'Textual Studies.'" *Proceedings of the Bibliographical Society of America* 99 (2005): 197–230.

Hunter, Dard. *Papermaking: The History and Technique of an Ancient Craft*. New York: Dover, 1978.

Jackson, Shelley. "Skin." 2010. http://ineradicablestain.com/skin.html.

Janowitz, M. "Sociological Theory and Social Control." *American Journal of Sociology* 81 (1975): 82–108.

Jefferson, Thomas. "Letters." http://press-pubs.uchicago.edu/founders /documents/amendI_speechs8.html.

Jensen, Kristian, ed. *Incunabula and Their Readers: Printing, Selling and Using Books in the Fifteenth Century*. London: British Library, 2003.

Johns, Adrian. *The Nature of the Book: Print and Knowledge in the Making*. Chicago: University of Chicago Press, 2000.

———. *Piracy: The Intellectual Property Wars from Gutenberg to Gates*. Chicago: University of Chicago Press, 2009.

Johnson, Reed. "The Unread: The Mystery of the Voynich Manuscript." *New Yorker*, July 9, 2013.

Kant, Immanuel. *The Critique of Judgment*. Translated by Werner S. Pluhar. Indianapolis: Hackett, 1987.

———. *Critique of Pure Reason*, edited by Paul Guyer and Allen W. Wood. Cambridge: Cambridge University Press, 1999.

Kaufman, Charlie. *Adaptation*. Dir. Spike Jonze. Columbia, 2002.

Keen, Andrew. *The Internet Is Not the Answer*. New York: Atlantic, 2015.

Keleman, Erick. *Textual Editing and Criticism: An Introduction*. New York: Norton, 2009.

Kephart, Rick." "Gregorian Chant Notation." N.d. http://bit.ly/1ev5rvm.

Keppie, Lawrence. *Understanding Roman Inscriptions*. Baltimore: Johns Hopkins University Press, 1991.

Ker, Neil R. *English Manuscripts in the Century after the Norman Conquest*. The Lyell Lectures. Oxford, UK: Clarendon Press, 1960.

Kindersely, R. "Standing Stones." *Letter Arts Review* 16, no. 4 (2001): 34–41.

King, Andrew "A Paradigm of Reading the Victorian Penny Weekly: Education of the Gaze and *The London Journal*." In *Nineteenth-Century Media and the Construction of Identities*, edited by Laurel Brake, Bill Bell, and David Finkelstein, 77–92. Basingstoke, UK: Palgrave, 2000.

Kramer, Ronald. "Painting with Permission: Legal Graffiti in New York City." *Ethnography* 11 (2010): 235–53.

Kuskin, William. *Symbolic Caxton: Literary Culture and Print Capitalism*. Notre Dame, IN: University of Notre Dame Press, 2008.

Latham, Sean, and Robert Scholes. "The Rise of Periodical Studies." *PMLA* 121 (2006): 517–31.

Leapman, Michael. *The Book of the British Library*. London: British Library, 2012.

Leedham-Green, Elisabeth, and Teresa Webber, eds. *The Cambridge History of Libraries in Britain and Ireland*. Cambridge: Cambridge University Press, 2006.

Lerner, Fred. *The Story of Libraries: From the Invention of Writing to the Computer Age*, 2nd ed. London: Bloomsbury, 2009.

Lessig, Lawrence. *Free Culture*. New York: Penguin, 2004.

Levinson, Paul. *Digital McLuhan: A Guide to the Information Millennium*. New York: Routledge, 2013.

Lewis, Danny. "Tsunami Stones." *Smithsonian*, August 31, 2015. http://www .smithsonianmag.com/smart-news/century-old-warnings-against-tsunamis -dot-japans-coastline-180956448/.

Lewis, Naphtali. *Papyrus in Classical Antiquity*. Oxford: Oxford University Press, 1974.

Lewis, Peter M., and Jerry Booth. *The Invisible Medium: Public, Commercial, and Community Radio*. Washington, DC: Howard University Press, 1990.

Liu, Alan. "Friending the Past: The Sense of History and Social Computing." *New Literary History* 42, no. 1 (2011): 1–30. doi:10.1353/nlh.2011.0004.

Liuzza, R. M. "Scribal Habit." In *Rewriting Old English in the Twelfth Century*, edited by Mary Swan and Elaine Treharne, 143–65. Cambridge: Cambridge University Press, 2000.

Loiperdinger, Martin. "Lumière's *Arrival of the Train*: Cinema's Founding Myth." *Moving Image* 4 (2004): 89–118.

Love, Harold. *The Culture and Commerce of Texts: Scribal Publications in Seventeenth-Century England*. Amherst: University of Massachusetts Press, 1993.

———. *Scribal Publication in Seventeenth-Century England*. Oxford: Oxford University Press, 1993.

Lunenfeld, Peter. *The Digital Dialectic: New Essays on New Media*. Cambridge, MA: MIT Press, 1999.

Lynch, Jack. *Samuel Johnson's Dictionary*. New York: Atlantic Books, 2004.

Lynch, Jack, and Anne McDermott, eds. *Anniversary Essays on Johnson's Dictionary*. Cambridge: Cambridge University Press, 2005.

Lyons, Martyn. *Books: A Living History*. London: Thames and Hudson, 2013.

Manguel, Alberto. *A History of Reading*. New York: Penguin 1997.

———. *The Library at Night*. New Haven, CT: Yale University Press, 2008.

Manly, John Matthews. "Roger Bacon and the Voynich Manuscript." *Speculum* 6 (1931): 345–91.

Marotti, Arthur F., and Michael D. Bristol. *Print, Manuscript, and Performance: The Changing Relations of the Media in Early Modern England*. Columbus: Ohio University Press, 2000.

Martin, Henri-Jean. *The History and Power of Writing*. Translated by L. G. Cochrane. Chicago: University of Chicago Press, 1995.

Martin, Lowell A. *Enrichment: A History of the Public Library in the United States in the Twentieth Century*. London: Scarecrow Press, 1998.

Marx, Leo. "Technology: The Emergence of a Hazardous Concept." *Technology and Culture* 51 (2010): 561–77.

Mauk, Ben. "Scattered Leaves." *New Yorker*, January 6, 2014. http://www.newyorker.com/currency-tag/scattered-leaves.

Mayor, A. H. *Prints and People: A Social History of Printed Pictures*. New York: Metropolitan Museum of Art, 2013.

McDermott, Joseph P. *A Social History of the Chinese Book: Books and Literati Culture in Late Imperial China*. Hong Kong: Hong Kong University Press, 2006.

McElligot, Jason. *Royalism, Print and Censorship in Revolutionary England*. Woodbridge, UK: Boydell Press, 2007.

McGann, Jerome. *Radiant Textuality: Literature after the World Wide Web*. New York: Palgrave Macmillan, 2001.

McGrath, Alister. *In the Beginning: The Story of the King James Bible and How It Changed a Nation, a Language and a Culture*. New York: Anchor Books, 2002.

McKenzie, D. F. *Bibliography and the Sociology of Texts*. Cambridge: Cambridge University Press, 1999.

McLaverty, James. *Pope, Print, and Meaning*. Oxford: Oxford University Press, 2001.

McLeod, Randall. "Gerard Hopkins and the Shapes of His Sonnet." In *VoiceTextHypertext: Emerging Practices in Textual Studies*, edited by Raimonda Modiano, Leroy F. Searle, and Peter Shillingsburg. Seattle: University of Washington Press, 2003.

McLuhan, Marshall. *The Gutenberg Galaxy: The Making of Typographic Man.* Toronto: University of Toronto Press, 1962.

Mehta, V. *Public Space.* London: Routledge, 2015.

———. *The Street: A Quintessential Social Public Space.* London: Routledge, 2013.

Miller, Paul, ed. *Sound Unbound: Sampling Digital Music and Culture.* Cambridge, MA: MIT Press, 2008.

Mims, Christopher. "Why Tablets Are the Future of Computing." *Wall Street Journal*, September 14, 2015. http://www.wsj.com/articles/why-tablets-are -the-future-of-computing-1442203331.

Minnis, A. J. *Medieval Theory of Authorship: Scholastic Literary Attitudes in the Later Middle Ages.* Philadelphia: University of Pennsylvania Press, 1988.

Montemurro, Marcelo A., and Damián H. Zanette. "Keywords and Co-Occurrence Patterns in the Voynich Manuscript: An Information-Theoretic Analysis." *PLoS One* 8, no. 6 (June 20, 2013), e66344. doi:10.1371 /journal.pone.0066344.

Morrissey, Lee. "Re-Reading Reading in Eighteenth-Century Literary Criticism." *College Literature* 31 (2004): 157–78.

Mott, Frank Luther. *American Journalism: A History; 1690–1960.* New York: Macmillan, 1962.

Mullaney, Thomas. *The Chinese Typewriter: A History.* Cambridge, MA: MIT Press, 2017.

New, Elizabeth A. *Seals and Sealing Practices.* Archives and the User 11. London: British Records Association, 2010.

Newman, Simon P. "Reading the Bodies of Early American Seafarers." *William and Mary Quarterly* 55 (1998): 59–82.

Nicolson, Adam. *Power and Glory: Jacobean England and the Making of the King James Bible.* London: HarperCollins, 2003.

Okasha, Elizabeth. "English Language in the Eleventh Century: Evidence from Inscriptions." In *England in the Eleventh Century*, edited by Carola Hicks, 333–45. Stamford, UK: Paul Watkins, 1992.

Oldenziel, Ruth. "Signifying Semantics for a History of Technology." *Technology and Culture* 47 (2006): 477–85.

Olguin, B. V. "Tattoos, Abjection and the Political Unconscious." *Cultural Critique* 27 (1996): 159–213.

Olmstead, A. T. "Darius and His Behistun Inscription." *American Journal of Semitic Languages and Literatures* 55 (1938): 392–416.

Olson, David. *The World on Paper*. Cambridge: Cambridge University Press, 1996.

Ong, Walter. *Ramus, Method, and the Decay of Dialogue*. Chicago: University of Chicago Press, 1954.

———. "System, Space, and Intellect in Renaissance Symbolism." *Bibliothèque d'humanisme et Renaissance* 18 (1956): 222–39.

———. "Writing Is a Technology That Restructures Thought." In *The Written Word: Literacy in Transition*, edited by Gerd Baumann, 23–50. New York: Oxford University Press, 1986.

O'Reilly, Tim. "What Is Web 2.0? Design Patterns and Business Models for the Next Generation of Software." *Communications and Strategies* 1 (2007): 17–38.

Orgel, Stephen. *The Authentic Shakespeare, and Other Problems of the Early Modern Stage*. New York: Routledge, 2002.

———. *The Reader in the Book: A Study of Spaces and Traces*. Oxford Textual Perspectives. Oxford: Oxford University Press, 2015.

———. "Textual Icons: Reading Early Modern Illustrations." In *The Renaissance Computer: Knowledge Technology in the First Age of Print*, edited by Neil Rhodes and Jonathan Sawday, 59–94. London: Routledge, 2000.

Orgel, Stephen, and Sean Keilen, eds. *Shakespeare and the Editorial Tradition*. New York: Garland, 1999.

Parkes, M. B. *Their Hands before Our Eyes: A Closer Look at Scribes*. London: Routledge, 2008.

Parkinson, Richard. *Cracking Codes: The Rosetta Stone and Decipherment*. Cambridge: Cambridge University Press, 1999.

Petrucci, Armando. *Public Lettering: Script, Power, and Culture*. Chicago: University of Chicago Press, 1993.

Pettitt, Paul, Paul G. Bahn, and C. Züchner. "The Chauvet Conundrum: Are Claims for the 'Birthplace of Art' Premature?" In *An Enquiring Mind: Studies in Honor of Alexander Marshack*, edited by Paul G. Bahn, 239–62. Oxford, UK: Oxbow Books, 2009.

Piper, Andrew. *Book Was There: Reading in Electronic Times*. Chicago: University of Chicago Press, 2013.

Pittock, Murray G. H. *Poetry and Jacobite Politics in Eighteenth-Century Britain and Ireland*. Cambridge: Cambridge University Press, 1994.

Plato. *Phaedrus*. In *Plato in Twelve Volumes*, vol. 9, translated by Harold N. Fowler. Cambridge, MA: Harvard University Press, 1925.

Powell, Barry B. *Writing: Theory and History of the Technology of Civilization*. Oxford, UK: Blackwell, 2009.

Price, Leah. *How to Do Things with Books in Victorian England.* Princeton, NJ: Princeton University Press, 2012.

Reddick, Allen. *The Making of Johnson's Dictionary.* Cambridge: Cambridge University Press, 1990.

Rheingold, Howard. "Virtual Communities: Exchanging Ideas through Computer Bulletin Boards." *Whole Earth Review* (Winter 1987). https://journals .tdl.org/jvwr/index.php/jvwr/article/view/293/247.

Roberts, C. H., and T. C. Skeat. *The Birth of the Codex.* London: Oxford University Press, 1983.

Robinson, Arthur H. "The Thematic Maps of Charles Joseph Minard." *Imago Mundi* 21 (1967): 95–108.

Robson, Eleanor. "The Clay Tablet Book in Sumer, Assyria, and Babylonia." In *Blackwell Companion to the History of the Book*, edited by Simon Eliot and Jonathan Rose. Oxford, UK: Wiley-Blackwell, 2008.

Roemer, Cornelia. "The Papyrus Roll in Egypt, Greece, and Rome." In *A Companion to the History of the Book*, edited by Simon Eliot and Jonathan Rose, 85–94. Oxford, UK: Wiley-Blackwell, 2009.

Rose, Jonathan. *The Intellectual Life of the British Working Classes.* New Haven, CT: Yale University Press, 2002.

Rose, Mark. *Authors and Owners: The Invention of Copyright.* Cambridge, MA: Harvard University Press, 1995.

Rosenheim, Shawn James. *The Cryptographic Imagination: Secret Writing from Edgar Poe to the Internet.* Baltimore: Johns Hopkins University Press, 1997.

Rossell, Deac. *Living Pictures: The Origins of the Movies.* Albany: State University of New York Press, 1998.

Rust, Martha. "It's a Magical World." In "The Page in Comic Books and Medieval Manuscripts," edited by William Kuskin. Special issue, *English Language Notes* 46 (2008): 23–38.

Saenger, Paul. *Space between Words: The Origin of Silent Reading.* Stanford, CA: Stanford University Press, 1997.

Said, Edward W. "The Problem of Textuality: Two Exemplary Positions." *Critical Inquiry* 4 (1978): 673–714.

Sanders, Clinton R. *Customizing the Body: The Art and Culture of Tattooing.* Philadelphia: Temple University Press, 1989.

Sanderson, George, and Frank McDonald, eds. *Marshall McLuhan: The Man and His Message.* Golden, CO: Fulcrum, 1989.

Schofield, Philipp, J. McEwan, E. A. New, and S. M. Johns. "Seals in Medieval Wales: 1200–1550." 2012. http://www.aber.ac.uk/en/history/research -projects/seals/.

Schreibman, Susan, and Ray Siemens, eds. *A Companion to Digital Literary Studies*. Oxford, UK: Wiley-Blackwell, 2008.

Searle, John R. *Intentionality: An Essay in the Philosophy of Mind*. Cambridge: Cambridge University Press, 1983.

Segaran, Toby. *Programming Collective Intelligence: Building Smart Web 2.0 Applications*. Cambridge, MA: O'Reilly Media, 2007.

Sherman, William H. *Used Books: Marking Readers in Renaissance England*. Philadelphia: University of Pennsylvania Press, 2008.

Shillingsburg, Peter. *From Gutenberg to Google: Electronic Representations of Literary Texts*. Cambridge: Cambridge University Press, 2006.

Siepmann, Charles Arthur. *Radio, Television and Society*. Oxford: Oxford University Press, 1950.

Signage Foundation. "Consumer Foundations of Retail Signage." N.d. Accessed November 24, 2016, at http://www.thesignagefoundation.org/Portals/0/Consumer%20Perceptions%20in%20Signage%20single%20pages.pdf.

Singh, Simon. *The Code Book: The Science of Secrecy from Ancient Egypt to Quantum Cryptography*. New York: Random House Digital, 2011.

Skilton, David. "The Centrality of Literary Illustration in Victorian Visual Culture: The Example of Millais and Trollope from 1860 to 1864." *Journal of Illustration Studies* 1 (2007). http://jois.uia.no/issues.php?issue=11.

Sliwa, Martyna, and George Cairns. "Exploring Narratives and Antenarratives of Graffiti Artists: Beyond Dichotomies of Commitment and Detachment." *Culture and Organization* 13 (2007): 73–82.

Smalley, Beryl. *The Study of the Bible in the Middle Ages*, 3rd ed. South Bend, IN: University of Notre Dame Press, 1983.

Smith, Margaret M. "Red as a Textual Element during the Transition from Manuscript to Print." In *Textual Cultures: Cultural Texts, Essays and Studies*, edited by Orietta Da Rold and Elaine Treharne, 187–200. Woodbridge, UK: Brewer, 2010.

Snow, Dean. "Sexual Dimorphism in European Upper Paleolithic Cave Art." *American Antiquity* 78 (2013): 746–61.

Sorkin, Aaron. *West Wing*. NBC, 1999–2006.

Stallybrass, Peter. "'Little Jobs': Broadsides and the Printing Revolution." In *Agent of Change: Print Culture Studies after Elizabeth L. Eisenstein*, edited by Sabrina Alcorn Baron, Eric N. Lindquist, and Eleanor F. Shevlin, 315–41. Amherst: University of Massachusetts Press, 2007.

Stam, Robert. *Film Theory: An Introduction*. Oxford, UK: Blackwell, 2000.

Stankiewicz, Mary Ann. "A Picture Age: Reproductions in Picture Study." *Studies in Art Education* 26 (1985): 86–92.

St. Clair, William. *The Reading Nation in the Romantic Period*. Cambridge: Cambridge University Press, 2004.

Steedman, Caroline. *Dust: The Archive and Cultural History*. New Brunswick, NJ: Rutgers University Press, 2002.

Steinberg, S. H. *Five Hundred Years of Printing*, 2nd ed. London: Penguin Books, 1961.

Sterne, Jonathan. *The Audible Past: Cultural Origins of Sound Reproduction*. Durham, NC: Duke University Press, 2003.

———. *Mp3: The Meaning of a Format*. Durham, NC: Duke University Press, 2012.

Suarez, Michael, and Henry R. Woodhuysen. *The Oxford Companion to the Book*. Oxford: Oxford University Press, 2010.

Summer, David E. *The Magazine Century: American Magazines since 1900*. Amsterdam: Peter Lang, 2010.

Summit, Jennifer. *Memory's Library: Medieval Books in Early Modern England*. Chicago: University of Chicago Press, 2008.

Susini, G. C. *The Roman Stonecutter: An Introduction to Latin Epigraphy*. Translated by A. M. Dabrowski. Oxford, UK: Blackwell, 1973.

Sutherland, Kathryn, ed. *Electronic Text: Investigations in Method and Theory*. Oxford: Oxford University Press, 1997.

Szirmai, J. A. "Wooden Writing Tablets and the Birth of the Codex." *Gazette du livre médiéval* 17 (1990): 31–32.

Tanselle, Thomas. *Introduction to Bibliography Syllabus*. Charlottesville: University of Virginia Book Arts Press, 2002.

Tettegah, Sharon Y., and Safiye Umaja Noble, eds. *Emotions, Technology, and Design*. Amsterdam: Elsevier Academic Press, 2016.

Thomas, Charles. *And Shall These Mute Stones Speak? Post-Roman Inscriptions in Western Britain*. Cardiff, UK: Cardiff University Press, 1994.

Thomas, Keith. "The Meaning of Literacy in Early Modern England." In *The Written Word: Literacy in Transition*, edited by Gerd Baumann, 98–131. Oxford, UK: Clarendon Press, 1986.

Treharne, Elaine. "The Architextual Editing of Old English." *Poetica* 71 (2008): 1–13.

———. "The Broken Book." November 23, 2013. http://historyoftexttechnolo gies.blogspot.co.uk/2013/11/the-broken-book-ii-from-book-of-hours.html.

———. "Fleshing Out the Text: The Transcendent Manuscript in the Digital Age." *Postmedieval* 4 (2013): 465–78.

Treharne, Elaine, and Greg Walker, eds. *Textual Distortion: Essays and Studies*. Woodbridge, UK: Boydell and Brewer for the English Association, 2017.

Trettien, Whitney. "Creative Destruction/'Digital Humanities.'" In *Routledge Handbook of Digital Medieval Literature*, edited by Jen Boyl and Helen Burgess. New York: Routledge, 2016.

Tufte, Edward. *The Visual Display of Quantitative Information.* Cheshire, CT: Graphics Press, 2001.

Turner, Fred. *From Counterculture to Cyberculture: Stewart Brand, the Whole Earth Network, and the Rise of Digital Utopianism.* Chicago: University of Chicago Press, 2010.

Twyman, Michael. *A History of Chromolithography: Printed Colour for All.* London: British Library, 2013.

UNESCO. "Convention on the Illicit Trafficking of Cultural Property." 1970. http://www.unesco.org/new/en/culture/themes/illicit-trafficking-of-cultural-property/1970-convention/text-of-the-convention/.

———. "Innovative Radio: Inspiring Social Change!" N.d. http://bit.ly/15SbLv3.

Vandendorpe, Christian. *From Papyrus to Hypertext: Toward the Universal Digital Library.* Translated by P. Aronoff and H. Scott. Champaign: University of Illinois Press, 2009.

Vander Meulen, David L. *Where Angels Fear to Tread: Descriptive Bibliography and Alexander Pope.* Charlottesville: Bibliographical Society of the University of Virginia, 1988.

van Dinter, Maarten Hesselt. *The World of Tattoo: An Illustrated History.* Amsterdam: KIT, 2005.

Veronis, J. *Parallel Text Processing: Alignment and Use of Translation Corpora.* Dordrecht: Kluwer, 2000.

Wainer, Edward. "How to Display Data Badly." *American Statistician* 38 (1984): 136–47.

Watson, Paula D. "Founding Mothers: The Contribution of Woman's Organizations to Public Library Development in the United States." *Library Quarterly* 64 (1994): 238–45.

Webb, Leicester. "The Social Control of Television." *Australian Journal of Public Administration* 19 (1960): 193–214.

Westrem, Scott D. *The Hereford Map.* Turnhout: Brepols, 2001.

Wiegand, Wayne. *Main Street Public Library: Community Places and Reading Spaces in the Rural Heartland, 1876–1956.* Iowa City: University of Iowa Press, 2011.

Williams, Linda, ed. *Viewing Positions: Ways of Seeing Films.* New Brunswick, NJ: Rutgers University Press, 1994.

Williams, Raymond. *Television: Technology and Cultural Form.* New York: Routledge, 2003.

Wood, James P. *Magazines in the United States.* New York: Ronald Press, 1971.

Woodmansee, Martha. "Genius and the Copyright." In *The Author, Art and the Market: Rereading the History of Aesthetics*, edited by Martha Woodmansee, 35–56. New York: Columbia University Press, 1994.

Yeo, Richard. *Encyclopaedic Visions: Scientific Dictionaries and Enlightenment Culture*. Cambridge: Cambridge University Press, 2001.

Yglesias, Matt. "Was *Paul's Boutique* Illegal?" *Slate*, May 7, 2012. http://slate.me/16uiIn2.

Page numbers in italics refer to figures.